The Legend of
HARLEY-DAVIDSON

The Legend of
HARLEY-DAVIDSON

PETER HENSHAW

STOEGER

Published in 2001
in the United States of America by
Stoeger Publishing Company
17603 Indian Head Highway
Accokeek
Maryland 20607
USA

ISBN 0-88317-230-5

Printed in Italy

ACKNOWLEDGMENTS
My thanks go to Garry Stuart, whose
superb pictures make the book what it
is, not to mention Tom Stevens for his
know-how where computers are
concerned, which can sometimes take
more understanding than Harleys. And
finally to Anna for her help and
support during the preparation of this
book.
Peter Henshaw
Somerset, England,
January 2001

The Legend of Harley-Davidson
represents the private view of the
author and is not an official Harley-
Davidson publication.

Contents

INTRODUCTION

What is a legend? According to a dictionary definition, it is 'a modern story that has assumed the characteristics of a traditional tale'. However, it may be going a little too far to describe any sort of motorcycle as legendary; after all, it's only a lump of iron, oil and rubber, however good it looks or inspirational it is to ride. And yet the term is applied to Harley-Davidson motorcycles more than to any others, and for many people, the myth is true.

In fact, the closer one looks at the Harley-Davidson story, the more the elements of the typical fairy tale reveal themselves: there are the aspirations of clear-thinking young men; the heights of achievement and the lows of depression; struggles in hard times; a long-running feud with an arch-enemy; and eventually, after a near-death experience, a return to power and success. Though a closer look at any motorcycle manufacturer with a long history will probably reveal similar ups and downs, for some reason it is the name Harley-Davidson that has achieved this special quality.

There are five chapters in this book which cover all the elements that have contributed to Harley's special status: each tells its own story, and all are elements vital to the history of Harley-Davidson's achievement. For the purpose of this book they are as follows:

First, *Roots:* the Herculean efforts of the initial founders, Arthur Davidson and William S. Harley, and how they were able to make the leap from two men working in a shed to owners of the largest motorcycle factory in the world – all in less than two decades. Second, *Motors:* there is one constant at the heart of the Harley legend from 1909 to the present day: a big air-cooled V-twin engine. This chapter chronicles the big twin in its seven forms to date, including all the successes and the failures. Third, *Racing:* how the company, a reluctant convert to racing, came to dominate this particular form of the sport, and still does today. Fourth, *Rebel Heart:* the image of Harley-Davidson, and how its bikes have come to be associated with rebellion. Finally, the *American Miracle*: this is the icing on the cake, and what finally turned the Harley-Davidson story into a legend.

In the 1970s, Harley-Davidson's bikes were not popular: they were regarded as outdated dinosaurs that vibrated and leaked oil. In the mid-1980s the company came within hours of bankruptcy. But now Harley-Davidson is on the crest of a wave, with worldwide record sales and a reputation to match. The story of how this incredible recovery occurred is told in the final chapter.

But of course, this is a legend that isn't over yet. What the future holds for Harley-Davidson, no one can really know, but if the next 100 years is as eventful as the first, there's a lot to look forward to.

How it all began: the original 1903 single, since restored by Harley-Davidson.

CHAPTER 1

ROOTS

How four practical men unknowingly gave birth to a legend

Did they know what they were starting? From left to right, William A., Walter and Arthur Davidson, with Bill Harley.

All legends have to start somewhere, and for Harley-Davidson this was in a garden shed in Milwaukee. It was here that William Harley and Arthur Davidson designed and built their first motorcycle. Did they know what they were starting? Probably not. In fact, the story goes that there was no notion of building the fastest motorcycle in the world, or the most exotic, or the most expensive, but one that simply worked; in fact, as the first nut-and-bolts prototype wheezed and wobbled its way onto the streets of Milwaukee, the stuff of legends was probably the very

last thing on their minds.

A student of Harley-Davidson's early years will notice that the character of the founders emerges quite clearly. There came to be four of them: Arthur, Walter and William Davidson, and Bill Harley. All were practical men with good solid engineering backgrounds and all were second-generation immigrants from working-class stock. The Harleys had originally come from Manchester, England the Davidsons from Aberdeen in Scotland, and by happy coincidence, both families found their homes close to one another

in Milwaukee. None of the four, until Bill Harley decided to take a couple of years out, had been to college, but all possessed a down-to-earth, conscientious attitude to hard work. They were innately conservative and cautious, unlikely to take blind leaps of faith without first carefully weighing all the pros and cons. And this conservatism was to be a characteristic of the company they founded right up to the present day. It has often been said that success is 10 per cent inspiration, 90 per cent perspiration: Bill Harley and the Davidsons are true exemplars of this philosophy.

First Prototype

Bill and Arthur both worked at the Barth Manufacturing Company in Milwaukee, Bill as a draughtsman, Arthur as a pattern maker. Shared hobbies had initially brought them together, notably fishing and cycling, as well as an interest in the internal combustion engine, unusual at the time, but part of everyday life today; but at the turn of the century it was an exciting new technology rapidly spreading into other fields.

It was no coincidence then, that in 1903, when the first Harley-Davidson motorcycle was sold, the Wright brothers were also testing their first powered aircraft and Henry Ford was unveiling his Model A. Neither was it a coincidence that all three of these engineering landmarks occurred in the United States. At the time, America was still a young country, offering a chance of a new life with hopes of prosperity for hundreds of thousands of immigrants a year. It was a melting pot of cultures, ideas and talents, a big country with rapidly improving roads and communications and a potentially huge market for long-distance transport.

But Harley and Davidson were less concerned with founding a dynasty than with tackling more immediate matters. Some say they decided to build a petrol engine to power their row-boat to better fishing grounds, others that it was intended for pacing cycle races. Whatever the reason, the two set to work with characteristic enthusiasm, enlisting the help of Emile Kruger, who also worked at Barth's and was familiar with the De Dion four-stroke engine.

Meanwhile, Walter Davidson, who was working as a machinist away in Kansas, had returned home to Milwaukee for the

wedding of his elder brother, Bill. Naturally, he was interested in the prototype motor, then still in pieces. The story goes that Walter watched in disgust as a hired hand butchered a prototype valve guide, so he rolled up his sleeves and took over the task himself. With his help, the first motorcycle, in reality the motor bolted into a bicycle frame, was ready to ride a few weeks later, in the spring of 1903. It was crude in the extreme, but it worked.

Measuring just 10 cubic inches (164 cubic centimetres), the motor's speed was controlled by changing the spark setting; in fact Ole Evinrude (another famous name, though not at that time) helped develop a working

carburettor. The inlet valve was opened, not by anything as sophisticated as a pushrod, but was sucked open by the descending piston. Power was not excessive, and vigorous pedal assistance was needed on all but level going. However, it worked.

Rather than rush headlong into production, the friends took their time to improve their prototype. In fact, there is little evidence that they regarded the motorcycle as anything but a diverting hobby, and all three kept their full-time jobs. But for a hobby, it was still being taken very seriously indeed: Walter returned to Milwaukee to spend all his Sundays and evenings on the project, while Bill Harley

designed a bigger motor of 25ci (410cc). It was in fact bigger than most contemporary engines, enough to push the bike along at 25mph (40km/h), which was too much for the flimsy bicycle frame, which began to crack and vibrate to pieces. The only answer was to produce a purpose-built frame: it still had pedals, a basic leather belt drive and no suspension, but the transformation from powered bicycle to motorcycle proper had begun in earnest.

Getting Serious

It was reliable too: that first 25-ci prototype was sold to a Mr Meyer, who rode it for 6,000 miles (9660km) before selling it on again; ten years later, the little

1909

bike had allegedly covered 100,000 miles on its original bearings. It simply underlined what Harley and the Davidsons were trying to do: build a simple, reliable machine that did its job.

Not all pioneer motorcycle makers were so conscientious. Many had more enthusiasm and grand ideas than common sense, more inspiration than perspiration. It was possible to buy motors and frames from a catalogue, bolt them together, sell the result by mail order and cross fingers. It was hardly surprising that most of these early entrepreneurs didn't stay in business for very long.

But for the young men of Milwaukee, things were just starting to happen. When, late in 1903, they received two orders for replicas of the 25-ci prototype, William Davidson Snr built a 10 x 8-ft (3 x 2.4-m) shed behind the family home on 38th Street and

Highland Avenue and rather significantly painted 'Harley-Davidson Motor Company' on the door. Maybe they were realizing it was a hobby no longer.

But still they took their time. Bill Harley decided to leave Barth's to take an engineering degree at the University of Wisconsin, supporting himself in the meantime by waiting at table. Over the winter, in his spare time, Arthur built up the first two bikes for customers, but it wasn't until 1905 that Walter finally left his job to work in the shed full-time. More orders came in, the shed was doubled in size, some help was taken on, and Arthur quit his day job.

More outgoing and gregarious than the others, he was a natural salesman. But rather than chase sales for their own sake, he began the painstaking task of recruiting dealers who could service the

bikes as well as sell them. This too set Harley-Davidson apart from many other pioneer manufacturers, who didn't much care how their bikes were sold, or relied on mail order and had no contact with customers at all.

Like many small companies, Harley-Davidson had insufficient capital to take advantage of the burgeoning demand for its product. Help came, however, in the form of James McLay, a rich uncle of the Davidsons, who loaned his nephews the money to buy a plot of land and build bigger premises. The story is often told how the new shed was mistakenly built encroaching on railroad land, until a few strapping friends of the Davidsons picked the whole thing up and shuffled it back 18 inches! And the place? Just off Chestnut Avenue, later renamed Juneau Avenue, where Harley-Davidson still makes

ABOVE
1909, and the very first V-twin. It didn't work too well, but better was to come.

OPPOSITE
Spot the difference? A restored 1906 bike is in the foreground with an 'in process' 1907 on the bench.

A 1910/11 single: note the belt tensioning device.

engines and gearboxes to this day.

Now the partners could really get down to business. In 1906 they built 49 machines in that first year at Chestnut Avenue. Quiet and reliable, with only minor changes since the 1903 prototype, it was advertised as the 'Silent Gray Fellow', due to its standard grey finish. It was reliability above all else that customers wanted, and production tripled to 152 in 1907, and tripled again the following year.

With the payroll expanding

and a second floor added to the factory, it was time to recruit a factory manager, and the eldest Davidson brother was the obvious choice. William was already a foreman with the Milwaukee Road Railroad company, with plenty of experience of managing men and machines. This was when Harley-Davidson Incorporated was born, with William as works manager, Arthur as sales manager, Walter as president and Bill Harley as chief engineer.

This was the nucleus of the

company that would see good times and bad for the next 30 to 40 years. Although the founders shared certain characteristics – practicality, common sense and caution – they also had complementary talents: Arthur the gregarious salesman; William the tough but fair workshop boss; Bill Harley the thoughtful designer; and Walter, who was the first official competition rider. In 1908 he won the Long Island Endurance Run on a Silent Gray Fellow, following it by achieving 188mpg (70km/litre)

on an economy run, both earning Harley-Davidson widespread attention. And the rapidly expanding company certainly needed all the success it could get. While Arthur carried on building up the dealer network, his older brother William was busy expanding the factory and hiring men to keep up with rocketing demand. William's son later recalled how he would install machinery and then start production as soon as the cement was dry.

The V-Twin is Born

Meanwhile, Bill Harley, having completed his engineering degree, was now ready to return to the fray with sleeves rolled up. Not that he had been idle while at college, where he had designed a set of leading link sprung forks. They were simple in principle, supported by four coil springs, but were strong, rigid and effective; unlike rival cartridge forks, they did not allow the wheelbase to alter as they worked. So attached was Harley-Davidson to this basic design that it stuck with it for the next 40 years, and even reintroduced it (in redesigned form) for the Springer Softail in 1989.

Back at Milwaukee, the search for new designs continued. Successful as it was, the Silent Gray Fellow had hardly changed since 1903, apart from a slightly larger engine, so for 1909 it became the

5-35, with a larger-still 35-ci (575-cc) motor, a longer wheelbase and larger frame. There was no gearbox yet – it kept the single-speed belt drive – but it could now top 50mph (80km/h); with basic suspension, just one rudimentary brake and skinny tyres, that was fast.

Not fast enough for some though, and the company was coming under increasing pressure to build a V-twin. That first attempt in 1909 was something of a flop, the company's first, and indicated that it had been ill-considered when compared with the single. Still, the second version of the F-head twin, in 1911, proved virtually trouble-free (see Motors, p. 27 et seq.). However, flop or not, sales continued to increase: they doubled to 1,000 in 1909, then tripled again the following year.

Even when the V-twin was finally in production, Bill Harley

An early 1912 single: by this time Harley-Davidson was increasingly concentrating on the V-twins.

ABOVE
One can understand why these
bikes were called 'Silent Gray
Fellows'.

RIGHT
A 1914 V-twin with the overhead-
inlet-valve, side-exhaust-valve
layout to which Harley remained
faithful for 20 years.

ABOVE
A 1913 Model 9-B single. It had chain drive at last, but still retained the pedals.

LEFT
From certain angles, the swept-back bars on early Harleys could look quite dashing.

1914 MODEL 10c SPORT

A 1914 single. The Harley-Davidson factory built over 16,000 bikes that year, taking care of the home market; meanwhile, Indian had succumbed to patriotic zeal and was concentrating on bikes for the military.

continued to experiment with new ideas. Harley-Davidson, along with most of the American motorcycle industry, enjoyed a brief period of innovation between 1910 and 1915/16, when it was developing faster than the equivalent European manufacturer. The reason was simple: to cope with the longer distances in America, US machines had quickly gained in power and size, so ancillaries such as transmissions also had to develop at a faster pace in order to keep up. In fact it was the transmission that saw the most radical change.

Bill Harley designed a basic

clutch for the rear hub (the company called it an 'idler') which allowed the rider to stop and start without lurching to a halt, then having to laboriously pedal-start the engine again. A proper multi-plate clutch, just as we know it today, soon followed, which in turn allowed the adoption of chain drive, and a three-speed sliding-gear transmission in 1915. Also in that year, the old drip-feed oiling systems were discarded in favour of an automatic pump on the twins, though a hand pump was still provided for nervous owners who didn't trust the new-

fangled 'auto' pump. A kick starter replaced the pedals and magneto electric lighting became an option. With typical attention to detail, the rear lamp was designed so that it could be removed and used as an inspection light, while a vacuum-operated switch made it impossible to walk off and leave the lights on.

In fact, from 1915 it could be said that the basic layout of the Harley-Davidson motorcycle had been established, and would stay that way for the rest of the century: 45-degree V-twin, chain primary drive, multiplate clutch, separate

gearbox, chain final drive, the latter replaced by toothed belts in the 1980s.

A dozen years after building their first prototype, the founders could look back with satisfaction, for their company was now a major player in the US motorcycle industry. There were many rivals (about 35 in 1913) but most were falling by the wayside, unable to compete on cost or quality. Indian was still the undisputed leader, but Harley-Davidson was catching up fast, Moreover, it was to receive a real boost as a result of the First World War.

When America entered the war in 1916, Indian joined in enthusiastically, turning over most of its production to military needs, which meant that there were plenty of disgruntled Indian dealers with no bikes to sell. However, canny Arthur Davidson, took advantage of this and lost no time persuading many of them to change sides. He had been careful to keep a decent slice of the production back for the civilian market, keeping Harley-Davidson dealers happy, which greatly strengthened the Harley-Davidson dealer network at Indian's

expense, and brought the fierce rivalry between the two companies into sharp relief. It was an unrelenting, often bitter, battle that lasted for 25 years, in fact, until Indian went bust, and was as active in motorcycle club rooms as it was in the companies' respective board rooms.

In reality, Harley-Davidson had done well out of the war, and this success encouraged the founders to forget their natural caution. They had borrowed the then-colossal sum of $3 million and expanded the Milwaukee works to a massive half-million

The 1915 Model 11F. The change knob for the new 3-speed gearbox is just discernible, introduced that year. The 'emergency' hand oil pump, to augment the auto pump, was another innovation for 1915.

17

There were acetylene lights on this 1916 Model F. However, the J was already available with electric lighting.

square feet (46500sq m). It was claimed to be the largest motorcycle factory in the world and in 1920 managed to churn out over 28,000 machines.

But the decade that had begun with such high hopes was proving problematical for the founders. First of all, the post-war boom developed into a slump and Harley-Davidson sales more than halved in 1921. Export sales had been a useful outlet (to 67 countries by that year), but as

times got harder, so import duties began to increase.

Meanwhile, the US motorcycle market was in long-term decline, with cheap cars replacing sidecar outfits as basic family transport. It was no surprise, therefore, that the company made its first-ever loss in 1921. Bearing in mind its large overdraft, Bill Harley and the Davidsons acted quickly. The factory was shut down for a month, all salaries wre cut by 15 per cent and the racing

programme was abruptly abandoned. Drastic action did the trick, but it would take 20 years for Harley-Davidson sales to match their 1920 peak.

First Flop

More heartache was to follow when after nearly 20 years of producing bikes that the buyers loved, Harley-Davidson produced its first serious flop. The Sport Twin was very different from the now traditional heavyweight V-twins. It was a smaller (37-ci/600-cc) horizontally-opposed twin, lightweight and easy to ride. It bore a resemblance to the English Douglas, and was an attempt to woo the man in the street, who would not normally have considered a motorcycle. Although up-to-date and trouble-free, the Speed Twin was not well received in its home market, though it did better in Europe and was dropped after a few years. However, in another attempt at diversification, the 21-ci (350-cc) side-valve and ohv singles were more successful.

If the founders hadn't already realized it, the failure of the Sport Twin rammed the point home. Times had changed since 1903: people weren't buying motorcycles as cheap transport any more, they wanted fast, exciting adrenalin-producing machines. It says much for their commercial acumen that the four, now approaching middle-age, responded by dropping the basic F-head single and introducing the Superpowered Twin, a 74-ci (1200-cc) version of the original 61. Not only that, but the almost legendary Two Cam V-twin was unveiled in 1928. It was advertised as, 'The Fastest Ever Model Offered by Harley-Davidson', which was true, and V-twin aficionados loved it.

But there were signs that Harley-Davidson's traditional attention to detail, to solid reliable machinery, was starting to slip. The new 45-ci (750-cc) V-twin of 1928 was a case in point. Fresh from the factory, it proved unacceptably slow, struggling to achieve 55mph (88km/h) or so when the Indian Scout was a 75-mph (120-km/h) machine and the Excelsior Super X even faster. A carburettor kit was hastily produced to improve matters, but the 45 was never a sparkling performer. It wasn't even reliable

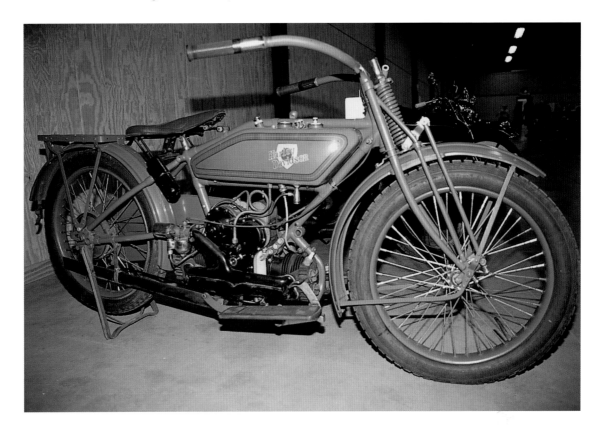

at first: the generator was mounted vertically (it was said that someone in the design department had forgotten to leave room for it) and its drive was prone to failure.

It says something for the company's sensitivity to these teething troubles that after some modifications had been made, in 1929, three second-generation Davidsons (Walter Jnr, Gordon and Allan) were dispatched on an 8,000-mile (13000-km) proving run on three new 45s. The young Walter, incidentally, was soon to take over publicity duties, including racing, while cousin Gordon became production manager, and demonstrates that Harley-Davidson was still very much a family firm.

As for the 45, in time it became a long-lived and thoroughly reliable part of the line-up, forming the basis of the later R- and W-series bikes, powering the wartime WLA and the evergreen Servicar.

A year after the 45, a new big side-valve twin was introduced,

but this too had its share of early troubles. There were some useful innovations on the new VL, like interchangeable wheels, a duplex primary chain and good electrics. But the early engine troubles were so serious that the factory was bombarded with requests to abandon its new side-valves and revert to the old F-head, especially the Two Cam. In other words, Harley-Davidson had produced two seriously underdeveloped bikes in quick succession; in spite of its success, its reputation of cast-iron reliability had been badly dented. These tribulations were bad enough, but in the next few years, the founders were to face a far more serious problem.

Hard Times
The Wall Street Crash of 1929 marked the end of a turbulent decade for the founders. It had started with a slump, and had progressed through ups, downs, and a general decline in the motorcycle market. And now here they were back at square one, only the situation was even more

The 1919 Sport Twin was Harley-Davidson's attempt to cater to the utility market. Sadly, Model T Fords already had that role well and truly sewn up.

ABOVE
A 1925 J-twin with electric lighting but still no front brake.

RIGHT
A 1927 F-head 61-ci (1000-cc) J-twin; only a year before, Harley had abandoned its inlet-over-exhaust engine for side-valves. Some enthusiasts were distraught!

severe. The effects weren't immediate: Harley-Davidson sold nearly 21,000 bikes in 1929 and over 17,000 in 1930. But sales dropped like a stone to 10,500 in 1931, less than 7,000 in 1932 (when over $300,000 was lost) and a disastrous 3,700 the following year.

As in the 1921 slump, the founders lost no time cutting costs. Anyone earning a salary of less than $60 a month took a 21 per cent pay cut, there were other cuts for the higher-paid, and hourly work was spread more thinly, to avoid layoffs. But it was not enough and redundencies followed soon afterwards, a bitter blow for those who had been with the company all their working lives. Office salaries of over $100 were cut by another 10 per cent and the four founders voted to cut their own incomes by half.

By this time, the founders were young men no longer. For 30 years they had worked long and hard to build up a successful business which had been no less than their lives' work. Though still losing money, after years of profits there was still a healthy surplus in the bank and Bill Harley and the Davidsons could have been forgiven for throwing in the towel. They could have sold the enterprise for whatever they could get for it, enabling them to settle back into comfortable retirement: closure of the business was certainly on their minds.

Just before Christmas 1931, Walter Davidson wrote a letter to the rest of the Board:

'There can be no question in anyone's mind that our business is showing a continual shrinkage ... Our foreign business has shown a very great decrease ... We then come back to the question as to whether this company can exist on the very decreased motorcycle business that we apparently face for

some time in the future ... With this greatly decreased business in sight it becomes the duty of our directors to decide what the future of our company is going to be.*

First, can we reduce our costs sufficiently to meet our decreased income and still make a profit?... At the present time we are in a wonderfully liquid position and certainly do not want to take our surplus that we have accumulated and dissipate it in losses in the next few years. If we decide we should continue in business, can the officers of the company honestly say to themselves that we can get our costs down to the point where we can show a profit?'

The key phrase is 'If we decide we should continue in business ...'. Well, they did continue, and it speaks volumes for the determination of the founders that they refused to take the easy option. They were rewarded with a small profit in 1933, when the giant Juneau Avenue factory was working at just 20 per cent capacity. The following

year, the recovery, slowly and painfully began. Not only had the founders agreed to carry on, they had also approved continued work and investment on a radical new model – the 61E Knucklehead.

Indian had also come close to disaster, but was saved by a takeover by the millionaire industrialist Paul du Pont. In the 1930s, the Harley versus Indian wars would get more bitter still: everything Harley-Davidson did appeared to be in direct response to its rival. Even the 45 and 74 side-valves had been a response to the fast and popular side-valve bikes that Indian was producing. In the early 1930s, Indian, with access to the du Pont chemical empire, introduced a range of bright new colours after decades of sombre greens and greys, and Harley followed suit.

The 80-ci (1310-cc) VLH of 1935 was in direct response to the 80-ci Indian Big Chief, and so on. In fact, it seemed as though Indian was making the running in all these innovations, with Harley-

One of the forgotton Harleys – a 1928 21-ci (350-cc) single.

RIGHT
The 1933 VL side-valve: note the Art Deco paint job.

BELOW
A 1938 UL side-valve twin, with Knucklehead styling and dry sump motor.

OPPOSITE
ABOVE: The 1936 ULH: 'H' stood for high-compression.

BELOW: The bike that changed the company: the EL Knucklehead shown here in 1940 guise.

Davidson following on. But even at the time of the fiercest competition, top management from both sides would meet every year 'in an atmosphere of strained conviviality', according to author Harry Sucher, to fix prices. It was illegal, but the arrangement suited them both.

But the Knucklehead changed all this. For the first time, here was a brand new Harley that was able to leap ahead of the opposition. It was fast, good-looking and up-to-the-minute – and it sold. Despite early troubles with oil leaks, not to mention a somewhat half-hearted launch by the company, the new bike was a hit, and its motor was a real milestone for the company (see p. 37 et seq.). It was so successful

The four founders started the Harley-Davidson Motor Company in a shed like this, which is in fact a replica, erected by Harley-Davidson outside its current headquarters.

that the following year the dowdy side-valves were all given the same flashy new styling as the Knucklehead. It also confirmed a final victory over Indian: Harley-Davidson now dominated the American motorcycle industry.

It's true that the Knucklehead made a huge impact, but right up to and into the Second World War the side-valve big twins remained Harley-Davidson's best-sellers. Meanwhile, the 45-ci (750-cc) engined Servicar continued to sell steadily and earn valuable revenue; the three-wheeler workhorse was so popular with the US police that it was still rolling off the production lines in 1972. During the war, of course, the WLA, the military incarnation of the original Forty-Five, was supplied in its thousands to the Allied armies. It still wasn't fast, but it was tough and reliable, quite good enough for the job.

All four founders lived to see their company survive the 1930s slump. Typically, none had opted for quiet retirement, and all were still involved in company affairs when they died. William Davidson died in 1937, having been ill for some time, ignoring medical advice to reduce his intake of good food and strong lager. It was his tight control of production that had allowed Harley-Davidson to expand rapidly in its early years, from half a dozen men in a shed to the biggest motorcycle factory in the world. Walter Davidson died in 1942, aged 66, followed in 1943 by Bill Harley, while Arthur, the consummate salesman, was killed in a car crash in 1950. So all four founders were no more: but their sons were waiting in the wings. The company their fathers had begun from nothing had survived war, competition and depression. Though they did not know it then, this came later to be regarded as the stuff of legends.

CHAPTER 2
MOTORS

The Why and How of the Harley-Davidson V-twin

One engine type dominates the Harley-Davidson story – the 45-degree V-twin. In fact, it is so connected with Milwaukee that one could be forgiven for thinking Bill Harley invented it. He didn't, any more than Honda invented the four-cylinder engine or Kawasaki the two-stroke. When Bill designed his first V-twin in 1909 (some say a prototype was built in 1907), he was behaving no differently from most of his contemporaries.

America's long straight roads soon revealed the inadequacies of the single-cylinder pioneer motorcycle, of whatever make. More power was needed, but bigger singles became increasingly difficult to ride and start, and vibration was a real problem. The answer was a V-twin – two singles mounted on a common crankcase and crankshaft in a 'V' formation. In theory it gave a near doubling of power for little more weight and cost. Better still, it would make use of existing tooling and fit neatly into the bicycle-derived diamond frame then almost universal.

In practice, Harley-Davidson's first attempt was a failure. The new engine was of 49ci (800cc), but it retained the automatic inlet valves of the single. Seven horsepower and a top speed of 65mph (105km/h) were claimed, but the automatic inlet valves, opened by engine vacuum rather than by a pushrod, limited engine speed to about 500rpm, so the twin turned out no faster than the single. Its power was just enough

The 1909 V-twin: not a success.

to make the leather drive belt slip, so it really gave the worst of both worlds. The first Harley V-twin was offered for a brief period in 1909, but swiftly disappeared from the catalogue.

The F-Head: 1911–1929

Harley-Davidson's first successful V-twin remained in production with few radical changes for 18 years, indicating that the company was not subscribing to change for change's sake. It was basically the same as the original 1909 twin,

but with two important updates. A belt tensioning device helped prevent slippage, and the overhead valves were opened by pushrods, rather than relying on engine vacuum. The latter allowed engine revs to venture up to four figures, so the V-twin was at last able to realize some of its power potential (6^1/$_2$hp was claimed). Like the first twin, and indeed all the early singles, this one used an overhead inlet valve and side exhaust – hence the term F-head.

At first, it carried over the first

twin's 49-ci capacity as well, but there was a 61-ci (1000-cc) option which was soon standardized; single-speed transmission was offered only for the first year. The introduction of a two-speed hub, and then a three-speed gearbox, was able to make best use of the F-head's power which, over time, gradually increased. Within a few years, Harley-Davidson was guaranteeing 11hp from every one off the line. The lubrication system was crude at first, though typical of its time. In the first year

A 1916 F-head board-track racer. Early racers used developed versions of existing motors.

A circa 1915 early V-twin. Positive operation of the inlet valves proved the key to making a workable V-twin.

of production, there was a gravity feed from the oil tank (one half of the fuel tank) down to the crankcase to service the crankshaft; it was then sucked up the cylinder walls and into the combustion chamber. Any excess was burnt off by the engine or drained out of the crankcase every now and then: it was a total-loss system in which one never needed to change the oil, as the engine drank it like gas! A magneto became available in 1915 to power the new option of electric lighting.

There were in fact several minor changes during the F-head's life, such as a four-lobe camshaft in 1917 (as used on the eight-valve racer) and from then until 1919, some 'fast' F-heads were built with greater precision, looser tolerances, to reduce the risk of seizure at high speed, and were bench tested. They were

LEFT
A 1929 three-cylinder 45 with vertical generator.

BELOW
The F-head developed into a reliable engine that served Harley-Davidson for nearly 20 years, and some riders for much longer.

The 1930 side-valve looked neat and compact but suffered from various teething troubles.

first named '500 motors', later 'E motors'. A larger 74-ci (1200-cc) version of the F-head followed in 1921, with increased bore and stroke and a larger 1¼-in (32-mm) Schebler carburettor.

The F-head's swansong was the almost legendary Two Cam, which appeared for the last two years of production. Two Cam racers had been around for several years, but these were road bikes, available in JH (61-ci/1000-cc) and JDH (74-ci/1200-cc) versions. There were two camshafts, with two lobes, each acting directly through tappets. They were much faster than the standard J and JD, and much loved by enthusiastic riders. For those that could afford it, a 61 in even higher tune was available, with 10:1 Ricardo cylinder heads

and a raging thirst for racing fuel.

The Side-Valve: 1929–1949

Controversially, Harley-Davidson replaced the long-running F-head with a side-valve engine. It did this because Indian and Excelsior side-valves performed so much better than the F-head; it was controversial because they turned out to be much slower than the opposition. The new 74-ci (1200-cc) VL side-valve V-twin shared its bore, stroke and capacity with the F-head, but otherwise was all-new. Harley-Davidson claimed 15–20 per cent more power than the F-head, but in reality it turned out to be just one horsepower. This wouldn't have mattered so much except that the new bike it powered weighed 120lb (54kg) more than the old one. In an

attempt to keep performance acceptable, the VL had been designed with relatively small, light flywheels. These allowed reasonably rapid acceleration up to around 50mph (80km/h), but performance then tailed off. The great drawback of light flywheels was that they robbed the big V-twin of its most precious asset – effortless, hill-climbing torque. They also allowed the engine to vibrate more.

The customers were horrified to see that their beloved F-head had been replaced by this inferior new motor, and there were loud calls for the old engine to be brought back. The complaints were so numerous that Harley-Davidson stopped shipping bikes out until improvements were made. There were other problems

A period-look 1933/4 VL: by this time its problems had been resolved. But a couple of years later, the Knucklehead was to point the way to a new era.

Tom Payne on his 1934 VLD. The big side-valve managed to secure an enthusiastic following of its own.

too, with broken or weak valve springs, clutch slip, difficult starting, and poor fit on the new splined hubs (designed to make tyre repairs quicker).

The engineering department went on a crash development programme to cure these faults. Stonger valve springs, a less sudden nine-spring clutch and a new starter ratchet were designed in short order. More substantial flywheels brought out the motor's torque, as did modified cams. Unfortunately, bigger flywheels needed bigger crankcases, which

in turn needed a bigger frame to accommodate them. Thirteen hundred VLs had to be completely rebuilt using this kit of parts, which cost Harley $100,000, and that was with the dealers doing all the work for free.

When all this work had been completed and the VL had finally settled down, its good points were able to shine through. Veteran dealers like Tom Sifton, accustomed to taking a group of customers on long, hot weekend rides, confirmed that the side-

valve V-twin had more high-speed stamina than the F-head, and that its ultimate top speed was slightly higher, at 87mph (140km/h). The side-valves were finally being accepted as Harley's standard big twin, even after the Knucklehead appeared in 1936; that was the Sportster, the side-valves were for traditionalists, tourists and sidecars. But a bigger 80-ci (1310-cc) version, Harley's biggest twin yet (and not to be surpassed in size until the Twin Cam of 1999) came along in 1935, and dry sump lubrication

The advent of the Knucklehead relegated the big flathead Harley to the role of long-distance tourer, a role it performed very well.

The 1938 UL. This is an 80-ci (1310-cc) version, the biggest Harley available at the time. Spotlights, panniers and luggage racks are all period extras.

1935 VLD Motor
On loan from John Parham, Anamosa, IA

from the Knucklehead finally
replaced the age-old total-loss
system a couple of years later,
along with the Knucklehead's
frame and more curvaceous
styling. The big side-valve Harley
survived the Second World War,
and was actually on offer as late
as 1949.

The Knucklehead: 1936–1947

The Knucklehead was a giant leap
forward for Harley-Davidson, a
long-awaited overhead-valve
engine that set new standards in
power and performance. For the
first time, it gave Harley a
technical lead over Indian, and
really marked the point at which
Harley-Davidson won the Indian
war. But it had been a long
process. The first drawings were
made in late 1931, and the bore
and stroke were decided: the
Knucklehead was to have a
shorter stroke than other big

ABOVE
The 1935 VLD motor, still with
total-loss lubrication.

LEFT
Although not everyone loved the
side-valve, it had more high-speed
stamina than the F-head.

Harleys to allow higher revs and more power. But work on the new motor then slowed, delayed by the very difficult trading conditions of 1932–33, when survival was higher on the list of priorities than exciting new engines. So it wasn't until the middle of 1933 that testing finally began, with the first complete bike not ready until May the following year.

Problems were immediately apparent, namely oil leaks from the many joints in the top end and an erratic oil pump which supplied too much lubricant to certain parts. The planned launch was delayed for a year, and even then Joe Petrali in the engineering department begged for more time to sort the engine out. He needn't have worried. The new 61E, as it was known, made a huge impact on excited dealers and enthusiasts. With its overhead valves and shorter stroke, it revved harder and made more power than any previous Harley, achieving 40bhp

ABOVE
The Knucklehead engine finally brought overhead valves to the V-twin.

LEFT
A 1940/41 Knucklehead FL, with its large buddy seat for two-up riding.

In its early years the Knucklehead was one of the fastest things on American roads. But this is a 1946 example, and it wouldn't be long before the drawbacks of the hand gearchange and heavy kerb weight became obvious.

at 4,800rpm, or twice that of the later F-head. The old sliding-gear three-speed gearbox gave way to a modern constant-mesh four-speeder, and the clutch was new as well. In fact, the complete machine was new, and it looked the part, with modern muscular styling that finally abandoned the spindly motorized bicycles of yesteryear.

Despite Harley-Davidson's desire for a low-key launch, it was emphasized to dealers that this was a limited-production model, and that no demonstrator machines would be allowed; however, the orders flowed in, and nearly 2,000 were sold in the first year. There were teething

troubles, of course: valve springs broke, and the early troubles of oil leaks and erratic oil delivery resurfaced. But, as with the side-valve twin, the engineering department worked overtime to overcome the problems, and made 100 changes to the engine in its first year. Like the side-valve, the new motor soon settled down to a reliable long run.

But it also changed Harley-Davidson's image: this was a performance bike, capable of an easy 90mph (145km/h); Joe Petrali underlined the fact by tuning one and taking it up to 136mph (219km) over a measured mile, and there were other speed and endurance records set by the new

bike. For Harley-Davidson, the Knucklehead was the start of a new era. It was also the first Harley engine to receive an unofficial nickname based on the shape of its rocker covers. According to one onlooker, they resembled a pair of bare knuckles: the name stuck.

The only major addition for 1941 came when a 74-ci (1200-cc) version of the Knucklehead was launched, said to be in response to police requests for more power. There was a new oil pump, but some early 74-ci crankcases cracked, causing a stronger version with longer reinforcing ribs to be quickly brought in, which was standardized for the 61 as well.

A Knucklehead, dressed to the nines with extra chrome and whitewall tyres.

The Panhead: 1948–1965

The Panhead was not a new engine. In fact it was really the Knucklehead with a few significant changes. But it looked very different, the rocker covers now resembling a pair of upturned frying pans. There were aluminium-alloy cylinder heads for cooler running, which had already been introduced on the side-valve twins, and promised to banish the overheating that sometimes affected the Knucklehead's cast-iron cylinder heads. Hydraulic tappets were an idea borrowed from the car industry, and promised quieter running and lower maintenance as they did away with the need for tappet clearance checks. In theory, the hydraulics should have provided more consistent valve clearances and timing.

In practice, they didn't, at least not at first. The problem was

ABOVE
The Panhead's neat pan-shaped rocker covers (hence the name) gave it a clean, uncluttered appearance.

LEFT
In its first year, the Panhead stuck with the old springer fork, but the Hydra-Glide was just around the corner.

By 1959, the Panhead had acquired rear suspension and had become the Duo Glide. It still had no electric start, but ...

... in 1965, that came too. This is an early Electra Glide.

that the hydraulic tappets were placed at the top of the engine, and the oil pump which supplied them was at the bottom. There were labyrinthine oil passageways in between, which played havoc with oil delivery and pressure and, as the oil was operating the valves, with valve timing and clearances too. The answer was to move the tappets from the top of the pushrods to the bottom, so that the oil had less far to travel: unfortunately, it took Harley-Davidson six years to make that change.

Another problem with early Panheads was related more to the customer than the company. In a bid to further reduce top-end noise, felt pads were stuck to the undersides of the large pan-shaped rocker covers, where they acted as dampers. They also helped lubrication by soaking up oil, then allowed it to drip steadily down onto the valve gear. Some owners, taking the rocker cover off for a look, as motorcyclists are prone to do, thought the felt was a factory mistake and ripped it out. The

result was less top-end lubrication and more noise!

But all these troubles were overcome, and the very clean-looking Panhead went on selling in steady numbers through the 1950s and early '60s (in 74-ci/ (1200-cc form only from 1953). There were also cycle part improvements around it, notably telescopic forks (the Hydra-Glide) in 1949, foot gearchange in '52 and rear suspension (the Duo Glide) in '58. The electric start Electra Glide appeared in the Panhead's last year, 1965.

A Hydra-Glide in all its glory. This was the first use of the 'Glide' name by Harley-Davidson, not to mention the telescopic forks.

ABOVE
A 1966 Shovelhead Electra Glide,
now with glass-fibre panniers
replacing the traditional leather.

RIGHT
The Shovelhead brought more
power, thanks to Sportster-style
heads.

OPPOSITE
A fully dressed Electra Glide from
1966. White seemed to be the
colour for accessories that year.

The Shovelhead: 1966–1983

For all its updates, the Panhead
was beginning to look
underpowered. Everything is
relative, and the 30 years since the
Knucklehead's launch had seen the
big twin transformed from a
genuine sports bike into a heavy,
soft tourer. It was now surrounded
on the home market by much
smaller, nimbler bikes which had
altered the world's perception of
how a motorcycle could be. More
power was needed, particularly to
overcome the extra 75lb (34kg) of
equipment which came with every
Electra Glide.

Like the Panhead, the new
Shovelhead was a development of
its predecessor, not a new concept.
So the 74-ci (1200-cc) V-twin kept
the Panhead's aluminium heads

ABOVE
The 1971 FX Super Glide, with the Shovelhead V-twin.

OPPOSITE
An AMF-era Super Glide: note the discreet 'AMF' badge.

and hydraulic tappets, but used Harley's experience with the overhead-valve Sportster engine to increase power. Using a Sportster-style top end boosted power to 60bhp, and it was raised again in 1968 when a Tillotson carburettor and improved porting took it to 65bhp at 5,400rpm. It certainly needed that extra horsepower, as a fully-equipped Electra Glide now weighed over 700lb (317kg), though stopping could be just as much of a problem. The Glide still relied on drum brakes, a cable-operated one on the front, hydraulic at the rear; disc brakes were still a few years away.

Unlike some of its forbears, the Shovelhead had no serious teething troubles; but being no more than a development of the original Knucklehead, by 1970 it was beginning to show its age. It still vibrated and leaked oil, traits which were becoming increasingly obvious in the face of ever more sophisticated rivals from Japan. But once again, Harley-Davidson was going through internal problems, and the Shovelhead had to struggle right through the 1970s, trying to

compete with machines like the Honda Gold Wing. It gained a capacity increase to the classic 80-ci (1310-cc) size in 1978, but that wasn't enough. As quality fell during the period when American Machine and Foundry (AMF) was running the company, buyers began to desert Harley-Davidson for something rather more reliable.

51

The Evolution: 1983–1999

The Evolution engine was another great leap forward, and the one that more than anything else helped to ease Harley-Davidson's fortunes in the 1980s. It was a long time coming: by the early 1970s, the Shovelhead was painfully outdated, but the Evolution project didn't even start until the mid-'70s, when incoming boss Vaughn Beals decided that what Harley needed was a product-led recovery. What with Harley-Davidson's manifold problems at the time, it took several years to reach production. And this was a motor originally seen as a stopgap; the role of Evolution, as an updated air-cooled V-twin, was to hold the fort until the all-new water-cooled NOVA family was ready. However, it was so successful that NOVA was forgotten, and the 'stopgap'

Evolution became the backbone of Harley's range for 16 years.

As the name suggests, Evolution wasn't new at all, but a development of what had gone before. It was still a 45-degree V-twin, air-cooled, with pushrods and hydraulic tappets; it even shared the Shovelhead, Panhead, and for that matter the side-valve's 80-ci capacity. But there was much that was new; in fact the whole engine, from the base of the barrels upwards. The Shovelhead's cast-iron barrels were discarded in favour of aluminium-alloy with iron liners. This alone saved 20lb (9kg) in weight, and of course they ran a lot cooler, which was just as well, as emissions legislation was encouraging manufacturers to run modern engines leaner, making them more prone to overheating. The cylinder heads were all-new,

LEFT
Evolution. This was the engine that helped turn the Harley-Davidson company around.

OPPOSITE
ABOVE: The Evolution was all-new, from the cylinder barrels upwards.

BELOW: Dyna Super Glide made good use of the Evo engine, as did almost every other Harley of the 1980s and '90s.

The Heritage Softail Nostalgia, a late Evo model.

with a narrower valve angle that allowed shorter, straighter ports. Underlining that torque, not power, was now the priority for Harley, the valves themselves were smaller, with milder timing and more lift.

But the new engine was higher-revving than the old, safe to 6,400rpm, thanks to the entire valve train – valves, pushrods, tappets – being lighter, and there were computer-designed cam lobes. It was stronger, too, with four long through-bolts holding each head and barrel to the crankcase, replacing the Shovelhead's separate fixings.

There were thicker con-rods to cope with the higher revs (ten times stronger, said Harley), and all-round closer tolerances. Oil drain was improved and a new two-stage advance curve improved the electronic ignition.

According to Harley-Davidson, the Evo produced 10 per cent more power than the Shovelhead and 15 per cent extra torque. More to the point, it had undergone 5,600 hours on the dyno and 750,000 miles (1207000km) of road testing before being passed for production. It was clean, reliable and didn't leak oil. At last, Harley-Davidson had designed an engine

that was right first time. There were rumours of a 95-ci (1560-cc) version in 1989, to counteract larger Japanese 'Harley clones', but high piston and bore wear in the prototypes apparently put a stop to the project. Fuel injection, probably a more worthwhile update, was made an option in 1995. Like its predecessor, the Evolution was beginning to look increasingly outdated when compared with the opposition; but what mattered was that it started first time, didn't leak, and sounded authentic. For thousands of riders, that was enough to ensure Harley-Davidson's survival.

The Twin Cam: 1999–

Every 15 to 20 years, Harley-Davidson feels the need to update its big twin. So 16 years after the Evolution was unveiled, along came the Twin Cam, which presumably will serve the company until 2015 or so. The name caused general excitement when it first appeared: could this be the first production Harley-Davidson with twin overhead camshafts?

It wasn't, and in fact at first glance the Twin Cam 88, as it was known, looked as if it had hardly changed. It was still an air-cooled 45-degree V-twin, with two valves per cylinder operated by pushrods. Many people were surprised at the engine's apparent conservatism, especially compared with the new Victory V-twin, which had twin overhead camshafts, standard fuel injection (an option on the Harley), oil-cooling and four valves per cylinder. It was also slightly bigger, at 92ci (1510cc), and had a lot more power. Both engines had been under development for several years, so it is unlikely that either company was unaware of what the other was doing. On the surface, the Twin Cam seemed to be even more of a gradual

'evolution' than the Evolution itself had been 16 years earlier!

But under the skin, nearly everything had changed. In fact, Harley-Davidson claimed that only 21 of the Twin Cam's 450 component parts were shared with the Evo, '... most of them screws. We've made improvements to virtually every part of the engine,' said Don Kieffer, director of programme management of the Twin Cam. He emphasized that sticking to an air-cooled pushrod format was deliberate policy, for definite reasons. 'What we didn't change is the fact that it is a 45-degree V-twin, air-cooled pushrod engine. These are the boundaries we set for the development of this new engine because they have been synonymous with Harley-Davidson since the first V-twin was developed in 1909.' Willie G. Davidson, now in charge of styling, speaking at the launch, confirmed how important was the 'feel' of the engine: 'We always walk a fine line between technical improvements and maintaining the look, sound and feel associated with Harley-Davidson,' he said. 'The new Twin Cam 88 is a great example of how we can successfully do this.'

So how was it new? Well, it was bigger, at 88ci (1449cc) the biggest engine ever built by the company. It had a bigger bore and shorter stroke (3.75 x 4in/95 x 102mm) compared to the Evo, allowing a slightly higher rev limit of 5,500rpm. There was a new single-fire ignition system, new intake and exhaust systems, a reshaped bathtub combustion chamber and a higher 8.9:1 compression ratio. A bigger air cleaner with front intake provided cooler intake of air. The result was 14 per cent more power than the Evo for the tourers, and 22 per cent more for the Dyna Glides. If that wasn't enough, the Twin Cam

The Twin Cam V-twin is Harley's current mainstay. It looks very like the Evo, but is really quite different.

New engines come and go, but the Electra Glide just keeps on going. This is a 2000-model Electra Glide Classic.

was designed from the outset to take a whole range of Screamin' Eagle tuning parts. A 95-ci (1550-cc) big bore kit, for example, was claimed to boost power by 6–8bhp, torque by 8lb ft.

Great attention was paid to cooling, this being one of the dwindling number of pure air-cooled engines available. The fin area was increased by 50 per cent, and the underside of each piston was cooled by an oil jet, said to reduce piston temperatures by 50°C. More strength was built into the Twin Cam, with the knowledge that many owners would opt for tuning parts. The whole unit was strengthened by a more rigid four-bolt connection between engine and gearbox;

unit-construction hadn't come yet, i.e. the gearbox was still in its own casing, making the whole assembly more rigid, and reducing stress on the primary drive. The crankcase itself was stronger as well as lighter, being high-pressure die-cast, and reshaped by changes in high stress areas: the advantages of computer aided design were making themselves felt. The redesigned tappet guide helped here: it was developed from that used on the recent Sportster, and also improved air flow and helped oil drain from the top of the engine. Inside, the con-rods were stronger than before (the 82-ci/1340-cc Evo had never been designed with a 95-ci hop-up in mind) and the flywheels,

now forged rather than bolted up, were stronger.

The two-cam assembly was new, of course, and was now driven from the crankshaft by a chain rather than a gear train, which reduced mechanical noise. Given the attention paid to banishing oil leaks on the Evo, there were plenty of improvements to the Twin Cam as well. An O-ring replaced the cylinder base gasket, while a metal-to-metal joint here was more stable with temperature fluctuations. At the top, the two-piece rocker box had fewer joints to leak, as well as making top-end maintenance easier, while the gaskets were of rubber-coated metal. The rocker boxes no longer had to help support the rocker arm shafts, which now had their own supports, and which also reduced noise. A new breather system and higher-efficiency oil pump improved lubrication, as did the filter arrangements: oil was now filtered *before* it was pumped into the engine.

The Twin Cam came with either carburettor or fuel injection, depending on the model; those who rode it agreed it was probably the best Harley twin yet. It was still underpowered compared to the opposition, but in Harley-Davidson's market, that mattered little to many riders. What they wanted was a V-twin that looked and sounded authentic, and that's what they got. Not everyone likes vibration though, and late 1999 saw the unveiling of the 88B. The 'B' stands for balance shaft, the first Harley so-equipped. There were two contra-rotating shafts, said to cancel out the big twin's vibration, and a ride on a 2000-model Deuce confirms that they do so very effectively. And so the Twin Cam carries Harley-Davidson into the 21st century: even with the radical new engine detailed below, it looks as if a 45-degree air-cooled pushrod V-twin will be part of the Harley line-up for a long time to come.

The Future: 2002–

In 2000 and early 2001, there were reports that Harley-Davidson was working on an all-new V-twin. As with the NOVA project, it had commissioned Porsche to develop the engine, though the difference was that this one looked far more likely to reach production. At the time of writing, it is still on the secret list, but from press reports and snatched pictures of the running prototype, some likely details can be gleaned. The engine is still a 45-

In this chapter only the core of Harley-Davidson's engine output has been detailed – the big twins. There were countless others, but none had the same importance and association with the name. Over the years, Harley-Davidson has made singles and flat-twins, two-strokes as well as four-strokes. It even toyed with the idea of a V4, while the shaft-drive flat-twin XA got close to civilian production in 1947; it is strange to think that Harley-Davidson came close to building a BMW lookalike, but it did. In fact, many of these forays into alternative engines were inspired by other companies: the 1920s singles and Sport Twin owed much to contemporary British practice; the little 7.6-ci (125-cc) Hummer of the 1950s was based on a DKW; that V4 was dreamt up by ex-Ace designer Everett de Long; and all the Aermacchi bikes of the 1960s and '70s were not even made in Milwaukee. Then there are the smaller V-twins, the 45-ci (750-cc) side-valve, and the Sportster in all its 55/67/74-ci (883/1100/1200-cc) forms. But none has been as central to Harley's history as the big twins. Except for the new Buell Blast, Harley-Davidson has stuck for the last 25 years to what it knows best.

ENGINE SIZES

Over the years, Harley-Davidson has appeared to favour particular engine sizes for its V-twins. Here is a summary, divided into the big twins and the early side-valves and Sportsters.

BIG TWINS

49ci (800cc)	61ci (997cc)	74ci (1203cc)	80ci (1340cc)	88ci (1449cc)
F-head	F-head			
		Side-valve	Side-valve	
	Knucklehead	Knucklehead		
	Panhead	Panhead		
		Shovelhead	Shovelhead	
			Evolution	
				Twin Cam

'SMALL' TWINS

45ci (750cc)	55ci (883cc)	61ci (997cc)	68ci (1100cc)	74ci (1203cc)
D/R/W sv				
K/KK sv				
	KH/KHK sv			
	Sportster '57–'71			
	Sportster 883			
		Evo '86 on		
		Sportster '72–'85		
			Sportster 1100 '86–'87	
				Sportster 1200 '88

degree V-twin, but there the similarity with all previous Harley-Davidson motors ends. It is liquid-cooled, with double-overhead camshafts and four valves per cylinder. There are thought to be two versions under development, a 61-ci (1000-cc) 100bhp twin, and a 92-ci (1500-cc) 135bhp version. Both will be fuel-injected and

come with an integral gearbox. It looks like a radical change for Harley-Davidson, though according to rumour, when the bike goes on sale in 2002, it will not be a replacement for any existing model. Instead, it will form the basis of a new range running alongside the old ones. Canny as ever.

CHAPTER 3
RACING

How despite itself, Harley-Davidson became a major force in racing

An early V-twin board-track racer. With no brakes and rudimentary safety equipment, such a sport was a risky business.

Place two motorcycle enthusiasts side by side in a bar, one English, one American, and ask them both the same question: Over the years, how well have Harley-Davidsons fared at racing? The Englishman will scoff and say that Harleys have never done well because they are too heavy, slow and cumbersome. But his American friend will know better. Harleys *have* done well at racing – on hill climbs, tarmac circuits and dirt tracks, drag racing and in endurance runs.

However, there is one

qualification: most of this success has been in the United States, with only very occasional victories in other parts of the world. On the dirt ovals, for example, that peculiarly American form of sport, the XR750 still dominates, 30 years after it first appeared. As a home-grown motorcycle, the Harley has done great things for American racing. That in itself has reinforced the strong association between Harley-Davidson and the USA, and made racing part of the Harley-Davidson legend.

Were they alive today, Bill Harley and the Davidson brothers would have been surprised at this turn of events. After all, their interests did not lay here, though Bill and Arthur had been interested in bicycle racing as young men. Their first motorcycle was designed to be solid and reliable, not to break speed records: the business of racing, with its attendant risk of breakdown, which would have done nothing to enhance their hard-won reputation, was safely left to others.

ABOVE and LEFT
These are 1915/16 factory racers, built when Harley-Davidson finally admitted to itself that an official racing programme was a good idea. The 'M' motor (above) is one of the original Wrecking Crew's engines. One careful owner?

Before the purpose-built eight-valve racer was unveiled, Harley relied on tuned versions of the standard F-head motor.

'A Needless Desire'

Endurance runs were a different matter. These were designed to test reliability, not speed, and accordingly Walter Davidson decided that he should enter a two-day event in June 1908, having already won a similar competition the year before. It started at Catskill, New York and finished with a 180-mile (290-km) circuit of Long Island. Eighty-four riders were flagged off at dawn, but by the end of the first day, half had been forced to give up when they encountered steep hills and rutted roads. But Walter not only finished, he also ended with a perfect 1,000-point score. He followed that up by winning an economy run on Long Island the next week, eking out fuel to

188mpg (70 km/litre). This was Harley-Davidson's first high-profile competition entry, and the resulting publicity was so good that it must have had an effect on the founders' attitude to racing.

Of course, private riders had been racing Harleys well before that, but solely on their own account. The early Harley-Davidsons were often slower than the opposition, but they tended to keep going after racier rivals had fallen by the wayside. This inherent toughness, rather than sheer speed, was to win Harley-Davidson many races in those early days.

But even after Walter's endurance victory, the factory was still reluctant to commit itself to racing. 'Race victories,' went an

official statement, 'are just a needless desire to impress and something a serious manufacturer has no need to do.' Harley-Davidson advertisements of the time emphasized not speed, but more practical virtues. 'This Harley-Davidson does the work of three horses', went one, 'It is the most comfortable ... most economical ... most reliable ... most durable ... easiest starting'. Nor did Harley wish to be associated with board tracks, the 'Thunderdromes' or 'Speed Bowls', the banked wooden circuits that were springing up all over the country. They allowed speeds of up to 90mph (145km/h), but were nicknamed 'Arenas of Death', because of the horrific accidents that occurred. Riders suffered

ABOVE
There are still no brakes on this J-series board-track racer, but there are open pipes, so bring your earplugs!

LEFT
Harley raced the little ones too. This is a 21.35-ci (350-cc) 'Peashooter' in race form.

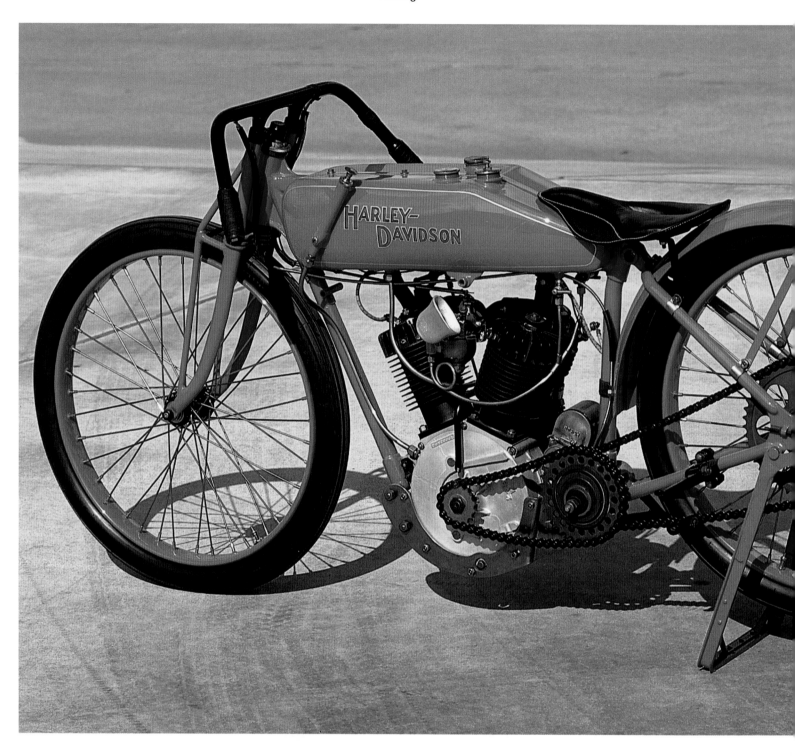

A 1920 61-ci (1000-cc) racer. What the production-based Harleys lacked in speed they made up for in reliability.

terrible injuries from splinters coming from the wood; in 1912 a bike spun into the crowd at Newark, killing spectators.

Safe, sensible Harley-Davidson wanted nothing to do with all this: but it could still quietly support some favoured riders, even to the extent of building race bikes for them, which happened as early as 1910. Indian, even then Harley's arch-rival, was receiving good publicity from racing, particularly

as a result of its one-two-three at the 1911 Isle of Man TT. So behind the scenes, Harley-Davidson was coming to realize that winning races sold motorcycles. In 1913 it took out a full-page advertisement featuring the following: 'Don't blame us when Harley-Davidson wins a race meet, because we do not believe in racing ... We build no special racing machines,' it added, 'but the results speak for themselves.'

Coming Clean

The decision to officially support racing had already been taken when that advertisement appeared. William Ottaway, who had done much to develop the racing Thor motorcycle, was taken on to do the same for Harley. At first, the agreement was to hot up Harley-Davidson's existing F-head V-twin, with no thought of producing special racing motors. The result was the II-K racer, with

ABOVE
A museum piece. A 1926 board-track racer in an 'authentic' setting. But would it really have been so spotless?

LEFT
Class C racing allowed the W-series side-valve to shine.

a tuned F-head, short wheelbase frame and 90-mph (145-km/h) capability. It failed to win in its first season, but by the end of 1914 was getting high placings. Meanwhile, the founders realized that to catch the very fast 8-valve Indians they would need something similar. So they authorized Bill Ottaway to design an all-new 8-valve bike – a purpose-built racer, rather than a modified road machine. With the

ABOVE
A WR racing on a typical dirt track.
Regarded as slow on the road, the
WR developed into a competitive
racer.

RIGHT
An early hill climber: note the
oversized rear tyre, with chains for
extra grip.

help of English engine expert Harry Ricardo, the Model 17 8-valve Harley was soon producing a respectable and reliable 50bhp.

But it wasn't until 1916 that the famous 'Wrecking Crew' appeared. The name was coined by a journalist for the way the official Harley race team simply wrecked the chances of the opposition. Although the line-up changed here and there, men like Jim Davis, Ralph Hepburn and 'Red' Parkhurst were always in the picture. They were good riders, and were backed by Bill Ottaway's new-found talent for team management: training, pit stops and tactics were all vital, and Ottaway made sure everyone knew it. He also ensured they

didn't rely on the 8-valve racer, which though fast still wasn't as reliable as the II-K. He would field teams of both: the tactics were for the 8-valvers to race off into the distance when the flag fell, tempting rival bikes into pursuit. When, inevitably, these bikes couldn't take the hot pace, the reliable old II-Ks were still there, ready to take the chequered flag.

All this worked: the Wrecking Crew won 15 National Championship races in 1916. In fact, the next few years were something of a golden age, with race after race falling to the men with the Harley-Davidson shirts. By the end of the 1921 season they held the 1, 5, 10, 25, 50, 100, 200 and 300-mile championships,

in other words, all of them.

But it was not to last. The sales slump of 1920 had caused Harley-Davidson to think again and to review its expensive racing programme (1921 alone had cost $20,000). At the end of the last race of the season it abruptly pulled out. The unlucky racers weren't even offered a ride home, but were left stranded in Arizona; some had to beg the train fare from a local Harley-Davidson dealer. It was a bad note on which to end that first run of success.

Production Racers

Through the early 1920s, private riders still raced Harleys; in 1923 Englishman Freddie Dixon took

WR 45s still race in classic events. This was Harley's standard race bike for nearly 20 years.

RIGHT
This is a 1956 KR, which took over from the WR as the official Harley racer.

BELOW
Aermacchis were raced too. This is a dirt-track specification Sprint.

LEFT
KRs were developed for road racing as well, though they faced tougher competition than on the ovals.

BELOW
XR750 – the standard Harley-Davidson racer from 1969 – also came in road-race form.

The Del Mar, California, mile-long dirt track: it's easy to see why American racers became masters of the high-speed slide.

the 1000-cc World Championship at Brooklands. But the American industry was really looking for a cheaper option and it came in the form of Class C racing in 1934. It was dreamt up by the American Motorcycle Association (AMA), the sport's governing body, and stipulated that bikes had to be production-based, not purpose-built racers, and 30.5-ci (500-cc) ohv or 45-ci (750-cc) side-valves. By this time, Joe Petrali was running the Milwaukee racing effort virtually single-handed. Joe was a talented rider and fine development engineer; it was his efforts through the 1930s that brought the Harley-Davidson racing victories, through both the little 21-ci (350-cc) 'Peashooter', which raced in AMA Class A, and racing versions of the 45-ci side-valve V-twin. So successful and widespread did Class C become, that Harley began to produce ready-made racers specifically for the purpose, such as the WR, WRTT and WLDR.

It gave a new boost to classic American dirt racing, which had grown out of the half-mile dirt ovals, which in the early days doubled as horse-race tracks. In European terms, it was very like speedway, with the riders deliberately sliding their machines around each end of the oval, but on bigger faster machines. This put high-speed machine control at a premium, and could be one reason why America has since produced so many world-class riders.

But Class C was not without its controversy. The allowance of larger engines for side-valve machines was intended to provide a level playing field for the smaller overhead-valve bikes. But it came with a limit on compression ratios: ohv bikes depended on a higher compression to make the most of

Scott Parker on an alloy-wheeled XR750 at the Del Mar track, California.

their more efficient, higher-revving motors. It reflected the fact that Harley and Indian had a great deal of influence with the AMA. They had funded it, and had saved it from bankruptcy, so it was not too surprising to find a set of rules that suited Harley and Indian 45-ci side-valve twins very well indeed.

None of this mattered so much in the 1930s, but after 1948, when racing resumed, a new wave of ohv British bikes, Nortons, Triumphs and Velocettes, began to compete in Class C. They were hampered by the rules, but sometimes still won because of their lighter weight and nimbler handling. The AMA refused to

change the rules, but Harley-Davidson still needed to find an answer to the Brits, and what it came up with was the KR of 1952.

It was of course a racing version of the KH road bike introduced the same year: Class C rules still insisted that the racers were based on production machines. So just as the K-series roadster had to use an outdated side-valve V-twin, so did the KR. However, those racing rules still allowed side-valve machines a big capacity advantage, and in the 18 years that the KR was Harley's official racer, it won the National Championship 13 times.

But the KR did not simply owe its success to favourable

rules. It had behind it a generation of side-valve tuning know-how. Harley-Davidson had been building side-valves for over 20 years, and both the factory and privateers, men like Tom Sifton, Len Andres and Ralph Berndt, knew how to get the most from of them: year after year, they would squeeze a little more power out of the KR. Cylinders were ported, cam profiles improved and double valve-springs fitted. The first factory bikes of the early 1950s produced 38bhp, but by 1969, when the KR was about to be superseded by the XR750, that had crept up to 64bhp.

Another strength of the KR

LEFT and BELOW
This XR is actually an ex-Jay Springsteen bike originating from 1980. Like almost every other Harley race bike, the XR had an unpromising start, but gradual development eventually transformed it.

A rare beast. This is a road-going VR1000, complete with lights, on show at the 95th birthday celebrations at Milwaulkee.

was its sheer adaptability. There was a huge range of options to suit different tracks and even different kinds of racing, for by now European-style circuit racing was creeping into the American calendar. The road-going KH had a modern swinging-arm rear suspension, but for dirt racing, a rigid rear offered better traction, so that's what the KR had as standard. However, the rigid rear was a subframe, which could be unbolted fairly quickly and replaced with a swinging-arm rear end if the circuit so demanded. Traditional dirt tracks didn't require brakes either, but these could be fitted to the KR if needed. There were 18- or 19-inch (46- or 48-cm) wheels and dozens of gearsets and sprocket options from which to choose; there were bigger tanks to suit longer races, plus seats, bars and fairings. When racing a KR, there may have been as much skill in setting one up for the circuit as riding it!

So the 1950s saw Harleys again dominating American racing; there was even talk of a new official Wrecking Crew. That never happened, but Joe Leonard won the National Championship on a KR in 1954, and Brad Andres took almost every round the following year, averaging 94.57mph (152.2km/h) at the Daytona 200. Joe Leonard retook the title in both 1956 and '57, by which time the Class C rules had been relaxed to allow a 9:1 compression ratio, which made the British bikes more of a threat. Meanwhile, Dick O'Brien had been made Harley-Davidson's race manager and was to be associated with factory racers for the next 25 years. The almost legendary Carroll Resweber then made the title his own for four years in a row, 1958–61. He might have gone on winning but for a racing accident, which badly damaged his leg.

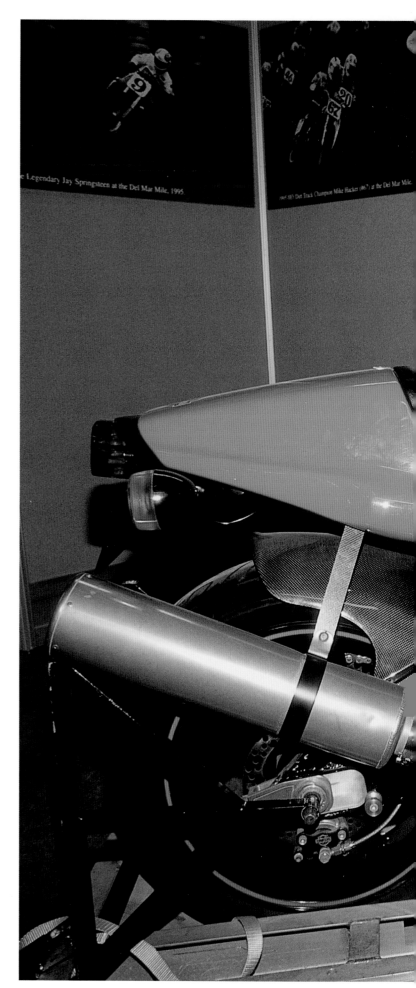

The Legendary Jay Springsteen at the Del Mar Mile, 1995.

1993 Dirt Track Champion Mike Hacker (#7) at the Del Mar Mile.

1995 Grand National Champion Scott Parker at the Del Mar Mile, 1995.

All through the late 1990s, various riders tried to take the VR1000 to victory, but none succeeded. This is Scott Zampach at Daytona.

Chris Carr was another rider who tried to get the best out of the VR1000.

Bart Markel took over the following year, though Harley actually lost the championship to Dick Mann on a Matchless G50 the year after that. But even that year wasn't too bad: it was the first of the AMA 250-cc Championship, and an Aermacchi-Harley (ridden by Markel) won it. In fact, the Italian-built Harleys in 15- and 21-ci (250- and 350-cc) form were to bring the company a brief spell of success in smaller classes in the early 1960s until the Japanese bikes came along.

But time was running out for the big KR as well. BSA-Triumph took the National Championship in 1967 and '68, and although a rider managed to get it back for Harley the following year, that was also the year that the old Class C rules were finally changed. Now side-valve and ohv machines both had the same capacity limit of 45ci (750cc), with no restriction on the number of cylinders. There was no way the old side-valve KR could compete and win under these rules, so Dick O'Brien and the racing department got straight on with the task of developing its successor, the XR750.

A (Dirt) Racing Legend

At the time, the XR was claimed to be all-new; but the bike that was unveiled in February 1970 was really a clever combination of existing and new parts. The quickest way to produce an ohv 750 was to take the club racing version of the Sportster and shorten the stroke to get it under 750cc (45ci). The result was bolted into the KR frame, cast-iron barrels and all, and it was a disaster. In the words of Harley historian Allan Girdler, it was 'overweight, underpowered and fragile'. The iron-barrelled motor overheated so regularly it was nicknamed the 'waffle-iron' and of

the 200 examples built to meet the rules, half were scrapped or dismantled. Not surprisingly, BSA-Triumph won the championship that year, and in 1971.

But better was to come. A 'Mark 2' XR750 with aluminium-alloy cylinder barrels defeated the overheating problem and boosted power. It won back the AMA plate for Harley in 1972, ridden by Mark Brelesford, while Cal Rayborn won three out of six of the Transatlantic race series in England that year, underlining both his riding skills and the fact that the XR750 wasn't just a dirt oval bike.

But it still wasn't a fairy-tale ending. Although the British factories were fading away, the Japanese now seemed determined to take their place by challenging Harley on its home turf. In the

coming years, both Honda and Yamaha were to find dirt-track success, while the XR750 was outpaced in open-class circuit racing quite early on. From the mid 1970s onwards, the XR750's success was largely restricted to its origins – the oval dirt tracks on which Harley had done so well for so long.

Meanwhile, Aermacchi had managed to come up with another world-class racer which was to repeat the early 1960s success of the 250 Sprint. Rider/designer Walter Villa masterminded the development of a new two-stroke twin, on which he took the 250-cc World Championship in 1974, '75 and '76, adding the 350 title in that final year. The following year, sadly, Harley-Davidson decided to pull out of Aermacchi

But while the VR was failing to deliver, many Harley riders were enjoying affordable racing on the 883.

altogether, and its brief spell of success in the smaller world classes was at an end.

As was remarked earlier, the XR750 was soon outclassed in circuit racing. That was true of the general classes, where it stood little chance against lighter, more modern machinery; but the story was different in the Battle of the Twins, where bigger Harleys were once again to find success on the tarmac tracks. This new race series was launched in 1981 to specifically allow the big twin-cylinder machines which some spectators loved to race competitively. It was a huge success, Ducati taking the first BOTT Championship. But Harley-Davidson under Dick O'Brien fought back with a bike whose reputation matched its name: Lucifer's Hammer.

This of course was a difficult time for the company, having just achieved independence but which was now heavily in debt. Lucifer's Hammer was a great morale-booster and became one of those legendary racers that deserves its own place in Harley history. There was nothing new or revolutionary about it: it was simply an existing road-race chassis fitted with an XR1000 motor. But tuned by Don Tilley to produce 104bhp, and ridden by none other than Jay Springsteen, it proved more than a match for the Ducatis, taking the BOTT race in 1983. That win, incidentally, also underlined Springsteen's riding talent, a man whose racing reputation and achievements were mainly confined to the dirt ovals. Yet here he was, racing and winning on tarmac. Dirt-based contracts prevented him from riding Lucifer's Hammer after 1983, but with Gene Church at the controls, and with sponsorship from HOG (the Harley Owners Group), it won the Grand Prix BOTT category in 1984, '85 and '86. In 1989, the Hammer was finally pensioned off, but its place in Harley history remains secure.

Ambition Thwarted

This success in specialist classes was all very well, but it is success in mainstream racing that really generates good publicity. Harley-Davidson wanted that mainstream success, wanted victories on the track to reflect its own miraculous recovery in the 1980s. So in 1989, just as Lucifer's Hammer was retiring, work started on an all-new race bike that would owe nothing to any previous Harley: the VR1000. It was to race in AMA Superbike and Grand Prix.

The signs were good. Many well-respected names from the world of Harley-Davidson racing were involved: Erik Buell, Jerry

Branch, Dick O'Brien, of course, and Don Tilley. Even Willie G. Davidson had a hand in the project designing the fairing; his son Bill was to later manage the race team. Technically, the VR was like no other Harley: a 60-degree water-cooled V-twin of 61ci (1000cc), each cylinder head with four valves and twin overhead camshafts. It had a short stroke and big bore for high-revving power (the rev limiter was at 11,000rpm); it had fuel injection and a balancer shaft. Ready to race in 1994, it produced 140bhp at 10,400rpm. There was an aluminium beam frame designed with the help of computer modelling after suggestions by Buell and a British company had been rejected. Suspension came from the well regarded Dutch firm of Ohlins, with 1.8-in (46-mm) inverted front forks. And the first person to race it would be Miguel DuHamel, son of the legendary Yvon.

But the debut race at Daytona 1994 was disappointing. At 355lb (161kg), the VR1000 was overweight, tipping the scales 20lb (9kg) over the minimum weight limit. Using magnesium crankcases would have cut that excess fat by nearly half, but it would have made the bike too expensive: as the VR wasn't based on a road bike, a certain number had to be built for sale to private customers, and magnesium cases could have made that uneconomic. As it was, a customer VR1000 would cost $50,000, plus the cost of racing parts if one actually wanted to ride it competitively.

Thanks partly to the weight problem, DuHamel found himself qualifying nearly eight seconds slower than the leading Ducatis. As well as being off the pace, the bike retired after 22 laps (less than half-distance) when a weld on the balance-shaft failed. Two weeks

later, in Phoenix, the VR again failed to finish. Frustrated by the setbacks, and despite some stirring rides, Miguel DuHamel left at the end of the year, leaving Chis Carr, a well known dirt-track rider, and Grand Prix veteran Doug Chandler to fly the flag. Slowly, the VR began to catch up, but it wasn't until 1998 that it became a serious contender. At Daytona that year, with Canadian Pascal Picotte riding, a poor pit stop kept Harley off the rostrum.

However, the honour of Harley-Davidson was about to be saved by a Japanese team. Takehiko Shibazaki built the all-black Daytona Weapon as early as 1992, as a follow-up to his own

version of Lucifer's Hammer. It used the familiar 45-degree air-cooled V-twin, tuned by Shibazaki in a Japanese Over frame. The bike didn't win straight away, but its team kept coming back with improvements. In 1997, Jay Springsteen won the F2 Daytona race on a Shibazaki bike with the unlikely name of 'Golden Balls'. And the following year, Weapon returned, and ridden by 'Mr Daytona' himself, Scott Russell, finally took the chequered flag.

It was Russell's fifth win at Daytona, prompting Harley-Davidson to sign him up to ride the VR1000 for 1999, confident that with the right rider it was now competitive enough to win.

But Russell didn't even make the start line that year: a bar room brawl the night before the race prevented him. Pascal Picotte took his place, but unfortunately crashed out. Also in 2000, Russell failed to give the VR1000 its coveted first at Daytona. The struggle for success goes on.

But if the VR1000 failed to live up to its promise, other areas of Harley racing were thriving. The Sportster 883 series, started by the company in 1998, was soon providing close, exciting racing all over the world. With only minimal modifications allowed, it was a relatively affordable way to race a Harley. In drag racing too, Harleys

continued to do well, the big V-twins often giving better results than revvier four-cylinder engines, with better traction off the line. But it is in dirt oval racing that Harley still rules supreme. Challenges from Triumph, Honda and Yamaha have come and gone, but the XR750 remains the ultimate oval racer. It is no longer possible to buy a complete new bike from the factory, but Milwaukee will still provide most of the engine and point you in the direction of people who can supply the other parts. And Jay Springsteen, more than 20 years on from his early successes, is still out there and riding. What is that if not a racing legend?

The 883 race series was popular in many parts of the world. This is the French Cup.

CHAPTER 4
REBEL HEART
How Harley-Davidson became the rebel's machine

Today, Harley-Davidson has a stronger image than any other motorcycle: stronger than Honda or Yamaha, even stronger than upmarket bikes like Ducati and BMW. And at the heart of this image is the rebel lifestyle. Like it or not, for the public at large and for many riders, a Harley is still the rebel's choice, beloved of the outsider. The company has embraced that image, adopted it as own, and made a great success of it. But it wasn't always so. At one time, Harley-Davidson attempted to distance itself from what it saw as the outlaw element, but now the idea is so central to the corporate image that top executives like Willie G. Davidson ride to rallies and mingle with the faithful dressed in jeans, bandannas and leather gear. Yet for its first 50 years, Harley-Davidson had a very different image: once it was the tourists' machine, a little slow, but solid and reliable. Of course, the touring culture of Harley-Davidson is still very much alive and kicking, especially in the USA, but it's no longer at the core of the phenomenon. So how did this turnaround happen, and why is the outlaw image so important to Harley-Davidson's current success?

This change of heart did not appear by magic, nor was it only associated with Milwaukee. In fact, there has always been a certain raffishness attached to all two-wheelers. Even before motorcycles hit the roads, early pedal cyclists had acquired a certain notoriety: in Edwardian England, cyclists were known as 'scorchers' or 'cads on castors'. Bicycles were some of the fastest things on the road, highly visible, their riders appearing to disregard other peoples' safety, not to mention their own. It took a while for early motorcycles to acquire the same image: after all, the first ones, little more than motorized bicycles, were designed to be practical rather than exciting. Their reason for being was that they offered personal transport for those unable to afford a car, and until Henry Ford got into his stride, that meant most people. Motorcycles, like step-through scooters in China and parts of the Far East today, were seen as practical family transport rather

80

trend by selling motorcycles back to the man in the street. It failed: what most American riders wanted were big, fast rorty V-twins. Thus was a pattern forming.

Tourists Come First

But alongside this obsession with speed, another side of the American market was developing. Then as now, America was a big country with straight roads, and long-distance touring was what many riders liked to do best. A big V-twin was perfect for the job: in the 1930s and '40s many touring clubs grew up to cater for tourists and there were various accessories designed to make distance riding more comfortable: panniers were a must, as was a good screen, and maybe a couple of spotlights. This was the beginning of the dresser style, which at the time was applied to both Harleys and Indians. Although, as will be seen, the outlaw image came to dominate the public conception of motorcycling, the tourists went on riding the roads of America right through the rest of the 20th century and beyond.

Even now, this fact is reflected in Harley-Davidson's range. The whole family of Electra Glides, Road Glides and Road Kings are all descendants of that style. The dresser image was to load the bike with extras: Harley-Davidson latched on to this, and from the 1980s began building bikes that were fully dressed for touring, straight off the production line, with hard luggage, full

How it all started: a late 1940s California Bobber, with high bars, chopped mudguards and high-level pipes.

than adrenalin machines.

But this soon changed. As cars became less expensive, so families increasingly preferred them over the motorcycle and sidecar. This happened first in the affluent USA, thanks to the inventiveness of Mr Ford, and was the reason why, by the late 1920s, only three major motorcycle manufacturers were still in existence: Indian, Excelsior and Harley-Davidson. Increasingly, motorcycles were bought, not from necessity, but from choice. They offered the speed, glamour and freedom that no car could, and nowhere was this more apparent than in North America. When Harley introduced its quiet, well behaved Sport Twin in 1919 it was attempting to reverse a

Early custom Harleys (this is a flathead example) were simple, reflecting the original intention to cut weight.

fairings, radios and every conceivable option. So the dresser is one of the three 'families' of Harleys still available now: sportster, tourer and custom.

It wasn't just the bikes that acquired a certain look to go with the touring image. Many touring clubs of the 1930s favoured a militaristic appearance for both riders and pillions. A typical ensemble was a peaked cap, smart twin-buttoned tunic, riding breeches and boots. The men wore ties, of course, and they could even be fined, albeit good-humouredly, for turning up for a run improperly dressed. This 'discipline' was reflected in the way they rode – in smart, tight formation – and in the use of 'ranks' in the clubs' organization.

This style lingered into the 1940s and '50s: a sociologist or psychologist would no doubt have had a field day theorizing as to why riders felt the need to conform to such a militaristic regime. Let's settle for the fact that they were just having fun.

If Harley-Davidson now capitalizes on the outlaw image, it once did the same where the smartly uniformed tourists were concerned. Look at Harley advertisements in the 1930s, '40s and '50s. The riders are wearing those boots and breaches, they are clean-cut and all-American. Emphasis was placed on the fact that motorcycling was a healthy active outdoor sport like any other. Women were often portrayed, to underline how

docile and easy to live with a Harley was; in fact, no one could have accused those early advertisements of sexism, so often were women shown in the driving seat! This was the image Harley intended to show the world and, by and large, it struck a chord with the general public, if bikes impinged on its consciousness at all. This was about to change.

It started in the late 1940s, with GIs returning home after fighting in Europe. They were still young men, but war ages people fast. They'd seen some terrible things, and returned to find that those who had stayed at home now had the best jobs, homes, wives and families. Like many returning soldiers, some

found it difficult to readjust to civilian life; they'd spent several years ruled by tight discipline, and felt they had earned their taste of freedom. Those who had learned to ride during the war did the obvious thing and blew their bonus on a motorcycle, and in 1946–47, that meant a Harley, or perhaps an Indian. To these men, the established touring clubs must have seemed not far removed from the US Army, with their uniforms, rules and tight rein on individuality.

So they formed their own, with names that reflected the way they felt: Satan's Sinners was one, Pissed Off Bastards another and the Hell's Angels would soon follow. Most of these were based in California; their favourite

ABOVE
Old meets new on this modern custom which mixes traditional Bobber looks with front disc brake, together with a modern paint job and large carburettor.

LEFT
Hell's Angels chapters are spread right across the world.

The Bandidos are lower profile than the Angels, but still very much a back-patch club.

weekend activity was to ride out of the city, raise hell in some small township, and ride home. As time went on, the clothes, language and culture of these clubs began to develop into a cohesive style.

They also modified their Harleys in the same sort of way. Most Harleys (especially the side-valves) were not fast, especially when compared with the British bikes that were just beginning to appear in the US in small numbers. Tuning was expensive, but a much simpler way to make a heavy Harley go faster was to simply dump some of its surplus equipment. So heavy front mudguards were discarded altogether; there were no screens or panniers and the rear

mudguard was shortened – 'chopped' or 'bobbed' – which gave this style of bike its name: the California Bobber.

The bobber, or chopper, as it was later known, became the motorcycle that symbolized rebellion. Nothing underlined more clearly the difference between the tidy tourists' clubs and this new breed of biker. They weren't too interested in upholding a fine image of motorcycling; they were more concerned with riding fast, making a great deal of noise and having a good time, and if this upset anyone, then that was too bad. Their bike of choice was the Harley-Davidson: not only was it available and relatively cheap, but it was a big tough bike which

could stand up to a lot of abuse. One could leave it outside all week, then jump on it come Saturday and do a 300-mile (500-km) run without a second thought. British bikes might be quicker through corners, but they seemed slightly effete, and needed more care and attention.

There had, of course, been a few wilder groups of riders before the war, though not on this scale. However, if it hadn't been for Hollister, maybe the new ones would have remained unnoticed by the rest of the world.

Nationwide Notoriety
Hollister is a small town in California which on 4 July 1947 was hosting a weekend of bike racing. It was an official, AMA-

ABOVE
Few Hell's Angels ride standard bikes.

LEFT
Sons of Silence is another back-patch club.

An English summer day and Hell's Angels are out there on the road.

approved meeting, and 3,000 respectable clubmen turned up to watch. They were joined by around 500 bikers who had less interest in the racing than in having a good time. According to *Life* magazine, the result was a full-scale riot by '4,000 members of a motorcycle club'. The front cover displayed a now-famous picture of a bike-slob sprawled across his Harley, beer bottle in each hand, while a cleaner-cut youth looked on. If the *Life* report is to be believed, the town was being besieged by a horde of hell-raising outlaws, no precious daughter was safe, and the American Way of Life was itself under severe threat.

The reality was less dramatic. The events took place one evening, but by noon the following day, just 29 cops had restored order. There were arrests, but these were for indecent exposure rather than for rape, pillage and murder. The reporting of the Hollister 'riot' smacked of media hype but, as in war, truth was the first casualty, as other papers, radio and TV picked up on the story. There were furious letters from irate motorcyclists in the following issue of *Life*, insisting that the trouble had been caused by a minority, and that it was unfair to tar all riders with the same brush. The AMA also leapt to the attack: it had long represented the acceptable face of biking, and emphasized that most riders had taken no part in the trouble: 'The majority of bikers took their sport seriously, and had parked their equipment and registered at local hotels for a good night's sleep. The rioters do not belong to any recognized motorcycle group.' These were, it continued, a tiny minority the 'one percenters'. The battle lines had been drawn, not only between outlaw bikers and the rest of

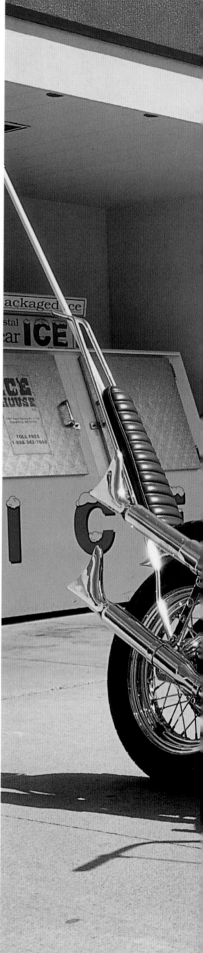

society, but also between outlaw bikers and the motorcycling establishment.

Predictably, this closing of ranks gave the outlaw clubs even more of a 'them and us' mentality, and caused them to knit more closely together. The Hell's Angels in particular began to organize themselves, as new groups sprang up across the country. In fact, the lurid media coverage was having the same effect: the publicity may have been making Middle America uneasy, but it was positively attracting a disaffected younger generation who saw no place for themselves in America's post-war prosperity.

The phenomenon really hit the mainstream with Stanley Kubrick's film, *The Wild One*, of 1953. The plot was openly based on the Hollister incident and features two rival gangs, led by Marlon Brando and Lee Marvin, who choose a small-town motorcycle race to air their grievances. The bad guys no longer rode black horses, but chopped bikes. (Brando actually rode a Triumph in the film, but the end result was the same.) The film was really offering a more subtle message than the simple 'bikers are bad', absorbed by many watching the movie, in which Brando portrays a confused rebel with a heart of gold. But he *is a* rebel, of that there is no doubt. 'What are you rebelling against, Johnny?' asks a

ABOVE
Chopper-style, with wide high bars.

ABOVE RIGHT
Two modern interpretations of the
original California Bobber style.

bar-room floozy. 'What have you
got?' he replies.

Like *Easy Rider*, 16 years later,
The Wild One made a huge
impact. From their West Coast
origins, outlaw bike clubs spread
rapidly across the country, into
Europe and eventually throughout
the world.

So what did they make of all
this at Milwaukee? At the time,
Harley-Davidson still regarded
itself very much a part of the
motorcycling establishment; it not
surprisingly sided with the AMA,
strongly denouncing the
protagonists at Hollister. In fact,
for years afterwards, some Harley
dealers refused to even service
bikes that had been customized in
the outlaw style. And right
through the 1950s and '60s,
Harley-Davidson refused to
weaken: it persisted in portraying

motorcycling as the wholesome
activity that had existed two
decades earlier. This was reflected
in the bikes they built; the big V-
twins offered a choice of sportster
or touring. As ever, the options
were practical components such
as luggage or a screen, certainly
no custom or tuning parts.

Rebellion as Fashion

But if Milwaukee chose to ignore
the outlaws, it didn't alter the fact
that it had inspired a whole new
movement of customization. As
the years progressed, the custom
Harley was evolving out of the
simple California Bobber.
Extended forks made their first
appearance in the 1950s, whether
in imitation of drag bikes (which
needed longer forks and frames to
keep the front wheel on the
ground) or in an effort to gain

more cornering clearance.
Whatever the motive, someone
realized that Harley springer forks
from the old VL were a good
inch longer than standard, so it
was an easy modification to make.
Then it was found that the
springers had the same cross-
section as the axle radius rods
from a Ford: given a competent
welder, it was therefore an easy
enough job to chop the forks in
half, weld in an extra piece of
metal and extend the forks by as
much as was required.

Jammer – a famous name in
custom circles – eventually offered
extended springers from 3-in (8-
cm) longer than stock to 18-in
(46-cm). An entire industry
developed as more and more
riders, whether true outlaws or
not, opted to chop their bikes in
the outlaw style. As forks became

ABOVE
A 1970s-style Panhead chopper with tiller bars.

LEFT
Early 1970s-style Sportster choppers were characterized by the extended forks and fat rear tyre.

Sonny Barger, the most famous Hell's Angel of all, standing outside the clubhouse of the Oakland Hell's Angels which, with others, he founded on 1 April 1957.

longer, they needed to be raked out at a wider angle to the ground to keep the bike on an even keel. Despite the arrival of telescopics, Harley's springer remained popular among the customizers; being mechanically simpler, it was easier to extend, and its spindly appearance suited the style of the stripped-down chopper.

As forks got longer, so other parts followed suit. The handlebars grew into buckhorn bars, then high risers, and finally ape hangers, the name of the latter originating from the long-armed position the rider was forced to adopt. Sonny Barger, founder member of the Hell's Angels, later recalled that a cheap way to fit high bars in the early days was by using the legs of a dining chair!

Meanwhile, the pillion's sissy bar grew ever skywards to match those tall bars. Big fat touring fuel tanks began to seem a little incongruous on these increasingly skeletal machines, and it was reputedly a racer named Billy Kuber who fitted a little 2.5-gallon (11.4-litre) tank from the 7.6-ci (125-cc) Hummer to his bike. Others followed, some with the tank from the Mustang scooter.

Now if Harley-Davidson and its dealers wanted nothing to do with outlaws and custom bikes, there were plenty of others happy to meet the demand. Custom specialists soon sprang up, offering ready-extended forks, ready to fit. Everything and anything that could be used to turn a standard, upright Harley-Davidson into a mean custom

machine could be bought off the shelf: complete frames (hardtail, plunger or swinging arm), handlebars, seats and headlamps. There were details like Maltese Cross rear lights or coffin-shaped fuel tanks; in fact, with pattern engine parts on sale, it was possible to build up an entire 'Harley' without using a single part made in Milwaukee. Eventually it was this wide proliferation of non-authentic parts in the 1970s that caused the company to clamp down on their supply .

The end result was the same: by the late 1960s, the typical chopper was a lean, spare and hungry machine. It was the personification of freedom, and a symbol of rejection of society's mainstream, and anyone leaving their bike as standard, or fitted

Hoggin' the bridge. A HOG (Harley-Davidson Owners Group) rally in the UK with over 1,000 bikes taking part.

RIGHT
The old and the new. A traditional T-shirted Harley rider on the left, white-collar weekender on the right.

BELOW
A HOG member displaying his collection of patches.

sensible touring accessories, was regarded as 'square'.

Easy Rider, the classic road movie of 1969, represented chopper culture at its peak; Peter Fonda's Captain America, a Panhead Harley in classic chopper style, became an icon for the decade. The bike that co-star Dennis Hopper rode was more radical, with short, straight bars, but it had the same effect. *Easy Rider* portrayed very different bikers to those of *The Wild One*, in which Brando and his fellows bikers are inarticulate rebels, possibly with hearts of gold but who are nonetheless looking for trouble. Fonda and Hopper were not: even though they are way beyond mainstream society, they are not fighting it. Their lifestyle may have seemed a little weird, but that was cool; all they wanted was to be allowed to get on with it. In *Easy Rider*, the biker had moved beyond the rebel phase to a laid-back, free-thinking hippy state; but his Harley-Davidson was

still central to his lifestyle. It was, as Harley's advertising slogan of the 1970s put it, 'The Great American Freedom Machine'.

Official Confirmation

At the time, Harley-Davidson was still officially ignoring what had become a huge part of motorcycle culture: the rebel image that existed alongside the custom bike. But even as *Easy Rider* was released, Harley-Davidson was developing its own version of the custom movement in which Willie G. Davidson's Super Glide of 1970 finally acknowledged what riders had been doing to Harleys for many years. It was the first factory custom and a huge success.

Of course, the Super Glide was not a strung-out chopper like Peter Fonda's, but a long and low drag bike imitator. Harley's chopper came in 1978 with the Low Rider, and by custom bike standards was mild; but the highish bars, stepped seat and sissy bar turned out to be exactly

A modern Evo chopper with Wide Glide-style forks. These days, customizers can do whatever they like – as long as they can afford it.

A 'digger'-style custom Harley in the 'Bay Area'-style of the late 1970s.

what many riders wanted: it was even more of a hit than the Super Glide had been, soon becoming Harley-Davidson's best-selling bike, apart from the basic Sportster. Willie G. (who became chief of the styling department) learned the lesson well, and many other custom Harley models followed. It is interesting, however, that the next one of any note, the Wide Glide of 1980, did encounter some boardroom resistance. Even after the success of the Super Glide and Low Rider, there still remained a fear that Harley-Davidson would be associated with the outlaw element of motorcycling, which of course still prevailed and was thriving. But it was too good a business opportunity to miss: the Softail (1986) mimicked older or custom-style hardtail frames; the Springer (1993) used an updated version of that much-extended springer fork.

Alongside the bikes, Harley-Davidson showed other signs of accepting the usefulness of its rebel image. There had long been official Harley clothing on offer, but it now began to reflect the biker look: lots of black leather, whether as jacket, leggings or chaps; bandannas, waistcoats and boots. Also, the range of official accessories began increasingly to reflect this image: higher bars, different pipes, new colour schemes, wheels, pegs, seats and lights. If that was all too much, one could just bolt on a 'Live to Ride – Ride to Live' air cleaner cover.

The Harley-Davidson Owners Group was the factory's official owners club, started in the 1980s. By happy coincidence, where street-level Harley ownership was concerned, its initials (HOG) bore all the right associations. The group was even organized into

'chapters', just like some of the outlaw groups: in fact, visit a HOG meeting anywhere in the world, and the no-nonsense black leather image abounds. A year's HOG membership now comes free with every new Harley, underlining the fact that it is not only a motorcycle that is being purchased but membership

of a new family, with its own brand of free-wheeling lifestyle.

In reality, the average HOG member could hardly be further removed from the real outlaw life, and can just as easily be a lawyer, teacher or computer programmer. Riding their Harley, in the company of like-minded folk, is a weekend thing, a form of relaxation from the hard-working

week; by Monday, it's off with the leather and back to the car. Some Harley riders still use their bikes as every-day transport: in fact they don't even wish to own a car. However, they are increasingly in the minority.

But for Harley-Davidson, this hardly matters. In fact, for any company, it's a very good position to be in. The Harley's image as a rebel's machine is now so strong that it looks like becoming thoroughly established. Take a look at TV and general media advertisements; whether the product in question is beer or jeans or hair gel, when the advertiser is set on suggesting a rough, freewheeling lifestyle, they wheel in a Harley-Davidson. Harley didn't set out to create this image, and for many years it tried to distance itself from it. But it has recognized the business sense of encouraging the myth, if not the reality, of the outlaw Harley. For thousands of riders all over the world, their Harley-Davidson is a statement of how they dream of living their lives, even if the job, mortgage and family makes this not quite possible.

CHAPTER 5

THE AMERICAN MIRACLE
Against the odds: how Harley-Davidson managed to survive

A 1955 KHK, the forerunner of the Sportster. But it wasn't enough to beat off the imported competition, and Harley's long decline into near-bankruptcy had begun.

Everyone was talking about the 'Japanese Miracle' in the 1960s and '70s. Here was a country that, just a few decades earlier, had been ravaged by war. It had been impoverished, occupied and humiliated, its industrial base all but destroyed; as a nation it would have seemed more feasible for it to have reverted to a peasant economy rather than to have achieved global economic power. But by 1970, it had made an astonishing recovery: it had full employment; many of its workers were well paid; its cars, radios and TV sets were being exported all over the world. Anything bearing the legend 'Made in Japan' was well-made, reliable, and relatively cheap. And nowhere was this more obvious than in motorcycles. The first to appear in the late 1940s were little more than crude motorized bicycles, the butt of jokes concerning frames made of bamboo. But the jokes stopped when clean, quiet, easy-riding Japanese bikes began to appear in America and Europe. BSA, Triumph, BMW, Harley-Davidson – all saw their traditional markets swallowed up or sidelined by Honda, Yamaha, Suzuki and Kawasaki.

It was a bad time for Harley. Take its traditional heartland, the US big bike market of 52ci (850cc) and over. For decades, it had dominated this sector, with no real rival. Even in 1973, it still commanded over three-quarters of such sales; but in 1981 it lost leadership of that sector to Honda. Two years later, less than one in

four big bikes sold in the US was a Harley. By 1985, the company was only hours away from liquidation, owing millions of dollars to the Citicorp bank. But by 2000, Harley-Davidson was riding the crest of a wave: it was building and selling more bikes than ever before, with 200,000 in that same year. It was making a profit and had waiting lists for its bikes which were being exported all over the world. And back in the US, it hadn't only regained leadership of that big bike market: in 2000, Harley-Davidson had also outsold Honda's entire range. Once again, Harley was the top-selling brand in the USA, bar none. However you look at it, this was a miracle of industrial survival, turnaround and transformation. How did it happen?

Post-War Optimism
The story really began after World War II, when Milwaukee again began to gear up for civilian production after five years devoted to the military. On the face of it, they were doing things right. A new production facility was opened to meet post-war demand, and sure enough, Harley-Davidson built more bikes per year in the 1950s than it had in the '30s. The 7.6-ci (125-cc) Hummer was introduced, a little two-stroke to encourage younger riders; the big twins weren't forgotten, and were gradually updated over the years: aluminium heads and hydraulic tappets in 1948, telescopic forks in 1949. Harley was a little late with

foot gearchanging (1952) and rear suspension (1958), but an electric start (1965) came before it was offered by the British.

In spite of all this, however, Harley-Davidson gradually lost market share through the 1950s and '60s, while production stagnated and exports dwindled to virtually nothing. The problem lay not in the traditional big twin; in many ways, it was still ideally suited to America's wide open spaces. And it still had a loyal core following, which bought 5–7,000 per year of the big FL and FLH right through the 1950s and '60s. But all round it, the American motorcycle market was changing: a big twin had once been the mainstream choice, but it was increasingly being sidelined into a niche market, and by 1965 Harley-

Davidson had a paltry 6 per cent of the overall US market. More and more riders were opting for the convenience of a Honda step-through or the exhilaration of a Triumph or Norton twin-cylinder sports bike. None of these imports could offer the long-distance comfort and stamina of a Harley, but they did attract a whole new generation of riders, the sort of people who would never have dreamt of buying a Harley.

Milwaukee's problem was that, despite the loyalty of its big twin customers, there just weren't enough of them to keep the company going. It was still very much a family firm, run in the conservative traditions of the original four founders. William Davidson had died in 1937, his brother Walter five years later and

Bill Harley followed the year after, while Arthur Davidson was killed in a car crash in 1950. Over this time, their sons had become well established in the business, and when Arthur died, his nephew William took over as president. Meanwhile, after a short tenure by Bill Ottaway (himself a long-serving employee), Bill Harley's son had already taken over engineering from his father. The board of directors was dominated by Davidsons and Harleys. It was a classic case of the family-run firm being strong on tradition, slow on change. To give an example, one proposal for an up-to-the-minute vertical twin to compete with the British imports came up for board discussion. It would have hydraulic forks, rear suspension and foot change; but it

never even made it to the prototype stage.

Not that Harley made no attempts at diversification from big twins. In fact, there were many, some more successful than others, but none was able to prevent the company's slide into takeover and eventually near-bankruptcy. We will examine these attempts in turn.

Half-Hearted Attempts

Harley-Davidson didn't actually design the little Hummer. It was a pre-war German DKW of basic design that was offered to Harley-Davidson as post-war reparations as a reward for its war work. It was simple in the extreme, a pre-mix 3-hp two-stroke with a three-speed gearbox and rubber-band front suspension. All Harley had

Three bikes that symbolized Harley-Davidson's dilemma in the 1960s: the Aermacchi Sprint (opposite below) was soon outclassed by the Japanese; the Sportster (opposite above) was overtaken in the horsepower race; and the Electra Glide (above) came to occupy an ever-smaller niche in an expanding market.

Traditional Harley riders were still by and large loyal to Milwaukee, but through the AMF years their patience was beginning to wear thin.

to do was bring it back into production and stick its own badge on it. Nor was it alone: all the Allies had had a crack at the DKW, and the Russians, Chinese and British (with the BSA Bantam) had all built their own versions.

At first, it sold well, with 10,000 in the first seven months of 1947, as William H. Davidson reported to his fellow directors. The trouble was that Harley-Davidson had failed to update it with the times. True, it did get telescopic forks later, and a capacity increase to 10 and 11ci (165 and 175cc), but that wasn't enough, with the result that the public gradually began to lose interest, and only 3,000 a year were being sold in the late 1950s. (BSA, it has to be said, made exactly the same mistake with the Bantam, soldiering on with the

same basic design for 25 years.) Harley didn't go that far, but even by 1960 it was clear that, next to the Japanese, this token small bike was outdated. Harley-Davidson did make one attempt to widen the Hummer's appeal. With one eye on the European scooter boom and another on cruder American versions like the Cushman and Mustang, it unveiled a scooter version in 1960. The Topper came in restricted (5-hp) and unrestricted (9-hp) form, both using the 165-cc two-stroke coupled to an automatic transmission. Unfortunately, it looked what it was – a heavy, clumsy afterthought; the American public was not impressed, and the Topper was dropped in 1964.

But what of the British imports, which had been selling in increasing numbers since the late

1940s? By 1950, imports were capturing 40 per cent of the US market, prompting Harley-Davidson to petition the White House for a tariff to be slapped on. It was turned down. The 31-/40-ci (500-/650-cc) Triumphs, BSAs and Nortons were slim, light and nimble. By contrast, the WL45 which Harley-Davidson offered was like a lumbering beast. It was a continuation of the pre-war W-series, with roots stretching back to 1928. Reliable, but heavy and slow, the 45 was stuck with an underpowered side-valve motor, a hand gearchange and antiquated suspension. As mentioned above, Harley-Davidson had already considered a fully up-to-date twin, but for reasons of its own never went ahead.

When the K-series was finally unveiled in 1952, it was

immediately apparent that it was old wine in a new bottle. And some of it was very new. The bike had a unit-construction engine/gearbox, telescopic forks, a swinging-arm rear suspension (six years before the big twins) and foot gearchange. Sadly, this up-to-date chassis housed a side-valve V-twin, which was an update of the original. So despite its new parts, the K-series was still heavy and underpowered compared with the opposition.

William H. Davidson was later to admit that the K-series had been a stopgap, designed to hold the fort until a more thoroughly up-to-date machine was ready. This is an odd explanation: the board had been discussing an overhead-valve 45 back in the 1930s, an ohv KL had already reached the prototype stage, and the K-series itself had taken seven years to reach production since the end of the war. The short answer is that the K-series was a missed opportunity which lost Harley-Davidson several years in its efforts to compete against imports.

But better was to come. The XL Sportster of 1957 was the bike the K should have been in the first place, with overhead valves and higher compression. In XLCH form it was at least as fast as any other production bike in a straight line, and it looked the part too, with its tiny fuel tank and staggered pipes; that XLCH look was to become the Sportster trademark for the next 40 years. It wasn't an immediate success, but Sportster sales grew gradually until it was outselling the big twins in the early 1970s. A second 'family' of Harleys had been born, distinct from the touring big twins, but just as much a Harley-Davidson for all that.

The Sportster was all very well, but despite being seen as the 'baby' Harley, it was still no

The 1971 Super Glide, with that infamous 'boat-tail' rear end.

competitor for the little Hondas and Yamahas. By the late 1950s, Harley-Davidson just didn't have the money, time or probably the expertise to develop a modern small bike of its own. So it imported someone else's, affixed its own badge to it, and bought 50 per cent of the Italian Aermacchi concern.

Aermacchi made a neat 15-ci (250-cc) four-stroke single, which was simple, light and handled well. Despite quality problems, the result of trying to run two factories separated by the Atlantic Ocean and a different language, the Aermacchi-Harley-Davidson Sprint sold quite well. It was followed by a 21-ci (350-cc) version, but by the early 1970s this pushrod single was really beginning to show its age. But it wasn't the only Aermacchi-built machine to cross

the ocean as a Harley-Davidson. There were 3- and 4-ci (50- and 65-cc) mopeds (yes, there really was a Harley-Davidson moped), a 6-ci (100-cc) enduro, a 125 commuter and finally a range of trail bikes in the mid 1970s. The final 7.6-, 11- and 15-ci (125-, 175- and 250-cc) Aermacchi Harleys looked the part, with oil injection two-stroke motors, five-speed gearboxes and trail bike styling. But problems of quality remained and they weren't cheap. Harley sold its stake in Aermacchi in 1978, to Cagiva. Never again would it lend its own name to another manufacturer's bike.

The AMF Era
The sad fact was that none of these bikes (Sportster apart) had proved a direct lifeline for Harley-Davidson. Despite increased

turnover (it doubled between 1958 and 1965) the company simply wasn't earning enough; by 1965 it had run out of money altogether, which was why it then offered its shares for the first time. It was careful to keep overall control (Harleys and Davidsons still held over half the stock) and new money did come in, to be spent on capital equipment and a major advertising campaign. In the short term this worked, and sales increased to over 36,000 the following year. But they fell the year after, and the year after that. Within a couple of years of the stock market flotation, Harley-Davidson was back to square one.

There was only one solution, and it must have been a painful one for those second- and third-generation Harleys and Davidsons struggling to continue what their forebears had begun: to sell the business. A company called Bangor Punta was keen, but was reputed to be an asset stripper; American Machine and Foundry (AMF), on the other hand, had a strong engineering base; it promised to allow the Harley-Davidson management to keep control; better still, its chairman Rodney C. Gott was a Harley-Davidson enthusiast. There was no argument, and Harley-Davidson became a subsidiary of AMF in January 1969.

With hindsight, it's easy to see that the promises that the old management would retain control were pie in the sky. Harley-Davidson was undercapitalized, inefficient and making too few bikes in an expanding market. The answer, according to Rodney Gott, was to boost production dramatically and fund new models from the resulting sales. So AMF's own York, Pennsylvania plant was converted to

motorcycle assembly, while the old Juneau Avenue factory in Milwaukee went over to engines and transmissions. Production was duly boosted, from 27,000 in 1969, to over 37,000 in 1971 and nearly 60,000 the year after.

But it was a nightmare: the York staff didn't have much experience of building bikes, and being 700-miles (1130-km) away from Milwaukee they had precious little opportunity to learn. Conversely, Milwaukee was resistant to change, and began to

resent the upheaval imposed from above. Tempers frayed and quality dropped like a stone. When Ray Tritten, a sort of AMF internal company doctor, was brought in to try and sort things out, he found that Harley was losing money on every bike it was making. There was a lack of professionalism in the engineering, marketing and spare parts departments; top management was complacent

concerning competition from Japan; there was wastage, bottlenecks and lack of proper forecasting. Five years after the takeover, AMF could have been forgiven for wondering why it had ever taken on the motorcycle business in the first place.

But even through these dark days of the 1970s, certain foundations were being laid for future prosperity. There were three men fundamental to the 1980s recovery, and two landmark motorcycles. The bikes came first.

In 1970, Harley-Davidson was about to have its production doubled by AMF, so it needed something new to help double sales as well. What it didn't have was the money or time to develop a new bike from scratch. The answer came courtesy of Willie G., a third-generation Davidson who had joined Harley-Davidson after working for Ford as a designer. He was a professional who happened to

In the 1970s, many owners of Electra Glides abandoned Harley in favour of the cleaner, quieter Honda Gold Wing.

have grown up around motorcycles, and he knew what certain Harley riders wanted most. They wanted a ready-made custom bike, which until then the company had been reluctant to produce. The new Super Glide filled the bill, with its long, low looks, flattish bars and lightweight front end; it owed much to the old stripped-down California Bobber. Better still, it cost very little to design and build, being a combination of the 74-ci (1200-cc) FL frame, engine and gearbox

significance for the future.

The Low Rider of 1977 performed the same trick again. As a custom bike, the Super Glide was pretty mild, but with the Low Rider, 'we took the custom bubble and pushed it further', as Willie G. said at the time. As the name suggests, the whole bike was squashed: the forks were lengthened and raked, the rear dampers shortened; there was a king and queen seat to give a low-riding 27-in (69-cm) saddle height; and flat straight bars

the flop of the XLCR. Unveiled in the same year, it was an all-black café racer-style bike, a mixture of Sportster and XR750 parts. But it was outsold by the standard Sportster six to one, and was soon dropped. The lesson was clear: buyers expected a Harley to look like a Harley, and nothing less would do.

So Willie G.Davidson was the first of three men instrumental in Harley-Davidson's recovery, and two of his most famous creations, the Super Glide and the Low

The 1998 XL1200 Sportster was no longer a sports bike in the modern sense of the word, but it now had its own faithful following.

with the Sportster's lighter-weight forks, 19-in (48-cm) front wheel and small headlamp. Lighter than a big twin, beefier than a Sportster, it completed the holy trinity of Harley 'families' – tourists, sportsters and customizers. Not only that, but it taught the company how easy it was to create a new bike (or what seemed to be one) simply by swapping around a few parts. This lesson was to have great

replaced the conventional buckhorns. It was a skilful blend of old and new, with instruments mounted on the classic Fat Bob tank and a 1903-style tank badge; but there were also alloy wheels and a twin-disc front end. The buying public loved it, and the FXS Low Rider outsold every other Harley, apart from the basic Sportster, over the next few years. In fact, it is interesting to contrast the success of the Low Rider with

Rider, clearly pointed the way to future prosperity.

But who were the other two? We left AMF man Ray Tritten wrestling with the problems of a company undergoing upheaval. One of the things he brought to light was that $10 million had been spent on developing a larger 67-ci (1100-cc) version of the Sportster V-twin – valuable time and money lavished on an engine that was already out of date. The

The Twin Cam Electra Glide Ultra Classic: part of Harley-Davidson's recipe for success was to offer bikes loaded with accessories, which in an affluent market certainly worked.

engineering department clearly needed a shake-up, and Tritten brought in Jeff Bleustein to do the job. Bleustein was AMF's chief mechanical engineer, a former professor at Yale who didn't have a motorcycle background but did have a very good track record in his profession. He changed the entire culture of the department, bringing in more highly qualified engineers. According to author Peter Reid, it took him two years to overcome the traditional Milwaukee way of doing things; but in the end, it paid off. Bluestein's rejuvenated engineers were to develop the Evolution V-twin, which carried Harley right up to 1999.

But Jeff Bleustein did not have overall direct control over Milwaukee. For that job, Tritten chose another AMF internee, Vaughn Beals. Like Bleustein, Beals didn't have a motorcycle background, but he was a good manager and understood what needed to be done to turn Harley-Davidson around. One of his first actions, in April 1976, was to take the top echelon of management away for a week of brainstorming at Pinehurst, North Carolina. Much came out of that meeting, but most important was that Harley-Davidson urgently needed new engines, in the short term, a much updated V-twin (this would be the Evolution); in the long term, a whole new family of engines to take Harley into the 1990s. The new engines were code-named NOVA, and a whole range was planned, from a 31-ci (500-cc) twin to 92-ci (1500-cc) six, all of

them water-cooled. To cut costs, they would share parts, and as Jeff Bleustein envisaged, the bikes they powered would be a radical departure from previous Harleys. 'The NOVA bikes were going to have a totally new look for Harleys, sleek and streamlined ... And they were going to be fast...'

AMF accepted the plan, and while Bleustein and his colleagues were busy developing the Evolution, the NOVA project was farmed out to Porsche. The parent company was to spend $10 million on NOVA, but by 1979, despite its best sales ever, Harley-Davidson was still only making very small profits. Meanwhile, Rodney Gott had retired and had chosen an accountant named Tom York as his replacement. However, York was less sympathetic to

Harley-Davidson, and saw more profit potential in other parts of AMF. He was adamant that AMF had had enough, and that the great white elephant Harley-Davidson should to be sold.

Flying Solo

To the outsider, things can't have looked that bad. Harley-Davidson may have lost police contracts, but sales were booming and 1980 saw the introduction of the Tour Glide. It still used the Shovelhead motor, but it was rubber-mounted to reduce vibration. There was a new, better-handling frame, five-speed gearbox and electronic ignition. Also that year came the FXB Sturgis, which threw out the chain in favour of a toothed belt drive. Both these innovations – rubber mounting and belt drive –

have been Harley features ever since, clear signs that the Bleustein engineering regime had been laying good foundations for the future.

Meanwhile, Vaughn Beals had been anything but idle. In late 1980, he wrote an internal paper recommending that AMF sell the company outright. When AMF bosses agreed to the idea, it turned out that he had a management buy-back scheme ready and waiting. The negotiations took months, but Beals managed to secure a large enough bank loan to buy Harley-Davidson from AMF: on 16 June, he and the new owners, which included Jeff Bleustein and Willie G. Davidson travelled from York to Milwaukee on a jubilant independence ride. Once again,

as an advertisement of the time put it, 'the eagle soars alone'. And the big bird arguably went solo in better shape that when it was under AMF's wing in 1969. The parent company had invested in new capital and plant, and Harley-Davidson was more modern and flexible than ever before. Turnover and capacity had rocketed.

But there were also 6,000 unsold bikes sitting in dealer showrooms. Harley-Davidson now owed $80 million to various banks; quality was still a major headache; and despite new bikes like the Tour Glide, Harleys were still outdated, many of them still vibrating and leaking oil. In 1981, the company lost its traditional lead in the US big bike market. In fact, the two years after buy-back

Road King, basically an Electra Glide without the fairing, is seen here with Twin Cam power.

107

By 2000, Harley's recovery was complete and customers were responding satisfactorily.

was Harley-Davidson's low point: it had lost a lot of money, and nearly half the workforce had been made redundant.

But in those two years, the foundations of recovery had been laid. Alongside the engineering improvements (Evolution had now got to the prototype stage), Harley-Davidson needed more efficient production methods. They came in three strands from Japanese methods, which at that time moribund industries in both Europe and America were seeing as a key to survival. The first of these was just-in-time inventory, which is now standard practice throughout the West. Instead of holding huge stocks of parts waiting to be used, getting rusty and obsolete, the company only held those parts immediately required to keep the production line going. This saved a lot of money. Employee involvement was the second strand: under

AMF, the shopfloor (at Milwaukee in particular) had had change imposed on it from above. Harnessing the skills of those who knew most about each job (i.e. the people doing it) boosted the drive for quality. And finally, every worker was given extra training so that they could monitor their own quality and output.

This all sounds deceptively simple, but in the long term it transformed quality, allowing Harley-Davidson to strive for what the Japanese called the ability to be 'right first time', instead of relying at the end of the production line on expensive rectifications by the dealer or under warranty agreements. Moreover, the company received a boost from outside. Twice before, in 1951 and 1978, it had asked the government to impose a higher import tariff on imported bikes, and both times it was refused. But in April 1983 a new tariff on

imports of over 43ci (699cc) was finally agreed. It was a high 45 per cent for the first year, gradually falling to zero over five years.

Tariffs weren't a magic solution, however: some Japanese bikes were downsized to 699cc to fit beneath the barrier, while Honda and Kawasaki already had US plants making big bikes, so they were unaffected. But it did give Harley a breathing space, and did mark 1983 as the company's turnaround year. This, of course, was also the year of the Evolution, which more than anything else must have underwritten Harley-Davidson's recovery over the next decade. Unlike some previous motors out of Milwaukee, this one really was right first time. It had already undergone 750,000 miles (1207000km) of road testing, and was quiet, clean and reliable. For the first time for a long time, people could buy a Harley knowing that it would always start and keep running, that it wouldn't vibrate their tooth fillings loose or stain their driveways with oil. The buyers responded: Harley had only 23.3 per cent of the big bike market in 1983, but that had crept up to 27 per cent by the following year. It was almost as if the riding public couldn't wait for an excuse to return to Milwaukee, and it did just that.

The Softail was another strong part of Harley-Davidson's product-led recovery through the 1980s. Harley-Davidson had already realized that people wanted Harleys to look like Harleys, not attempts to compete head-on with the Japanese. The Softail, which cleverly hid its rear suspension units horizontally under the gearbox, had the look of a traditional hardtail rear end with at least some modern comfort. In reality it had a mere 3in (7.6cm) of suspension travel, but that was

enough for many people. The story goes that Harley-Davidson didn't invent the Softail at all; a man named Bill Davis had built one, which Vaughn Beals spotted at a bike rally and liked what he saw. He was impressed, bought the patent, and it has been part of the Harley line-up ever since; in fact, it was the best-selling model for some time. The point was well made: the new, or returning, breed of Harley buyers had no use for a modern-looking bike, they wanted a piece of rolling nostalgia with all the modern conveniences besides.

A Close Call

But incredibly, just as the recovery was gathering pace, Harley-Davidson came closer to bankruptcy than ever before. It still owed millions to the banks, and in 1985 Citicorp, one of the main lenders, announced that it was pulling out: it wanted its money back. Things were going

well, but Harley-Davidson still didn't possess that kind of cash. Just days before the 31 December deadline, Vaughn Beals, Richard Teerlink and Tom Gelb managed to secure replacement funds from Heller Financial. Even after the deal was agreed, there was a last-minute panic to get the right signatures on the dotted line; being New Year's Eve, many of the key people were away from home. Teerlink managed to persuade Heller Financial to wait just a little longer; if they hadn't, the deal would not have gone through in time and Harley would have had to file for protection under Chapter 11 in US law, or face liquidation. It was a close-run thing.

Now the recovery could get underway in earnest. Harley-Davidson was still heavily in debt, but that was about to be solved forever. It did the same thing that had been tried in the 1960s –

The Heritage Softail became one of Harley-Davidson's best-selling bikes, reflecting the feelings of nostalgia for the way Harleys used to look.

raised money on the stock market by selling shares. With the company in its darkest hours, this would have been a disaster: who would have wanted to buy into a firm that was on the slippery slope? But now, quality, market share and sales were all improving fast, and everyone seemed to know it. By 1986, the Harley-Davidson recovery was a high-profile affair: it seemed that here at last was an American company that could compete with the Japanese on its own terms. So the share take-up was enthusiastic and a lot of money – $90 million – rolled in as a result. Not only was Harley-Davidson able to substantially reduce its borrowings, but it was able to spend a $50 million surplus buying Holiday Rambler, a maker of motorhomes. Of course, it could have spent the money revitalizing the NOVA engine programme, but Rambler made more business sense, and making motorhomes meant that Harley-Davidson no longer had all its eggs in the motorcycle basket; it could retain customers who had decided they were too old for bikes. In any case, it was by now clear that Harley customers didn't want streamlined water-cooled NOVA bikes; they wanted air-cooled, V-twin Harley-Davidsons.

Moreover, there was still money to develop the existing range. The Sportster got an 54-ci (883-cc) version of Evolution in 1985, and a 74-ci (1200-cc) the following year. The company showed canny marketing in resisting the temptation to climb ever upmarket with more expensive bikes; there was always a stripped-down low-priced Sportster 883 to attract new riders into Harley ownership. In 1989 the Springer Softail was unveiled, matching the hardtail look rear end with a set of springer forks that looked very much like Bill

Harley's 1907 originals. Like the Softail, it didn't have the comfort of conventional modern suspension, but it looked the part, and that's what buyers wanted.

In fact, it seemed that Harley-Davidson could do no wrong: it made over $17 million profit in 1987, $27 million the following year and $59 million the year after that. Comparing the end of the 1980s to the beginning underlines the point: productivity was up by half; inventory cut by 75 per cent; scrap/rework down by two-thirds; and it had regained its lead in the big bike market, capturing almost 50 per cent. Things were going so well that, a year ahead of schedule, Harley-Davidson asked the government to remove the tariff on imported bikes. This wasn't quite as magnanimous as it sounds: duty was already down to 15 per cent; but it was a publicity coup, and underlined the impression that Harley-Davidson had returned in style.

Ever Upwards ...
The 1990s saw more of the same. Production, sales and profits just went on rising, but any new bikes were variations on the same theme. Sportsters apart, every bike in the range used the 82-ci (1340-cc) Evolution engine with five-speed gearbox and belt final drive. Fuel injection came late in the decade, and then only on selected models, while the Twin Cam engine, which replaced the Evolution in 1998/99, was another air-cooled pushrod V-twin.

It bears repeating that Harley-Davidson customers wanted their bikes to look, sound and feel like old Harley-Davidsons, and nothing else would do. This is illustrated by the contrasting fortunes of the FXRT and the Fat Boy. In the early 1990s, the FXRT was Harley's nearest thing to a modern bike: rubber-mounted engine, modern

fairing, air-adjustable forks and twin front disc brakes. It was lighter and easier to ride than the touring FLs. A police-specification FXRP had been instrumental in persuading many police departments to give Harley-Davidson a second chance. But a mere 600 civilian FXRTs were sold in 1990, and the bike was dropped three years later. The Fat Boy, on the other hand, had a solidly-mounted engine, despite Harley's excellent rubber mounts having been around for a decade. It had soft suspension and little cornering clearance. But it was a huge success, and is still part of the line-up ten years later. And, of course, what people liked about the Fat Boy was the way it looked: the solid disc wheels, all-silver colour scheme and twin 'shot-gun' pipes. They liked it because it looked like a big, solid, 'fat' Harley.

Harley-Davidson wasn't just selling to enthusiasts with rose-tinted spectacles either. Harley-Davidsons, more than at any time in their history, had become fashionable. Sylvester Stallone, Bruce Springstein and Mickey Rourke were all happy to be seen as Harley-Davidson owners. Not for nothing was America's movie capital now known as 'Harleywood'. Not only were the bikes appearing in advertisements, they were also helping to sell everything under the sun, proving that there is no better testament to a strong public image. To the general public, a Harley-Davidson was authentic: it had street credibility and no-nonsense appeal. Many motorcyclists knew that the average Harley was heavy, slow and cumbersome compared with any modern bike; but in the scientific microchip age, it was a reminder of simpler times that millions found irresistible. It got to the point where Harley-Davidson could launch a special edition of

the Heritage Softail called 'Nostalgia', and still be taken seriously.

Perhaps it was the fact that its image had become so important that Harley-Davidson began to register certain names. From now on, no one would be able to use the term 'Glide' or 'Sportster' or 'Hog' – they were all Harley-Davidson trademarks. Most bizarre of all was the attempt to patent the distinctive exhaust note of the 45-degree V-twin. However, after several years of courtroom wrangling, Harley-Davidson at last threw in the towel.

But it wasn't all image, and there were some new bikes in the 1990s. The Dyna Glide of 1993 was an update of the FXR, still with a rubber-mounted engine, but with a redesigned frame to make it look solid-mounted. The basic 883 Sportster finally acquired belt drive and a five-speed gearbox that year, but retained its low price. The

following year, the Road Glide appeared, a sort of stripped-down tourer that owed much to the basic FL Electra Glide; a quick-release screen replaced the fairing, and the speedometer was moved to a traditional tank-top nacelle. Fuel injection arrived in 1996, not to improve power, but as a response to emissions regulations, though there were many side benefits. Fuel economy and cold starting were improved, and there was a diagnostic function. There were also a couple of bikes in the late 1990s to give a more sporting image: the Sportster 1200S had extra power and twin discs, while the Dyna Glide Sport featured adjustable suspension. But by modern sports bike standards, these were still cruiser bikes for Harley, the Buell being its true sporting division. Then there was the T-Sport of 2000, basically a Dyna Sport with panniers and a small screen, an ostensibly sports-

touring Harley. However, it wasn't a sports-tourer by any stretch of the imagination.

As ever, what Harley-Davidson did best was to keep on producing nostalgic variations on the themes of the big twin and Sportster. And the new Twin Cam V-twin which first appeared in 1998, and had spread across the entire big twin range by 2000, was a case in point. It didn't have twin cams, or water-cooling; some versions were still fuelled by good old-fashioned carburettors. Outdated from new? Yes, but intentionally so, as there was no need to tamper with a thoroughly successful formula. In the mid-1990s, Harley announced it would be increasing production to 200,000 by 2000. It managed it too. As we progress into the next century, with sales breaking all previous records, it's clear that the Harley-Davidson legend is very far from over.

A road-going limited-edition Twin Cam Road Glide, painted in traditional orange, black and white.